WHAT PEOPLE ARE SAYING ABOUT *50 GOLDEN RULES*

"A timely reminder that, as entrepreneurs, we never stop learning. Garry has created a brilliant and comprehensive guide to growing and scaling a business. I love how you can dip in and out of relevant chapters depending on the most pressing challenge within your business at that time. The book is packed full of useful frameworks, personal suggestions and easy-to-follow bullet points; it's like having your own non-exec with you all day, every day."

– Nathan Lomax, Entrepreneur,
Investor and Founder of Quickfire Digital

"Nine out of ten new businesses fail, but nine out of ten that receive the correct advice succeed. This book is full of just the advice you need to succeed."

– Geoff Burch, The Alternative
Business Guru and legendary Speaker.

"I wish I had access to this book when I started my own business. It would have saved me time and money, which I was short of at the start."

– Mark Schenkius, Founder
and Owner, ROI-10

"*50 Golden Rules...* provides a one-stop shop for any entrepreneur, new or experienced. It will give you novel or refreshed insights to help you along the ever-winding road to successful business building. A must-have."

– Paddy Lawton, Multiple exited Entrepreneur, Founder of Fact360

"*50 Golden Rules: The Beginner's Guide to Entrepreneurship* is a practical guide on becoming a successful entrepreneur and a must-read for anyone that wants to start their own business or make their current business more successful."

– Don Klock, Former CPO Colgate-Palmolive, currently Professor of Supply Chain Management, Rutgers University

"I wish I had read *50 Golden Rules* twenty years ago; it is a great distillation of entrepreneurship pearls of wisdom from someone who has lived and breathed the issues discussed. Of value to anyone involved in early-stage ventures, there are loads of practical tips, and useful resources in the appendices, all described clearly and concisely in convenient bite-size sections. Thoroughly recommended."

– Struan McDougal, Managing Director, Cambridge Capital Group

"An absolute treasure chest of business insights and ideas to ease and constantly re-set the entrepreneurial journey. From now on, this is my silent NED."

– Martin Avison, Founder, AngelGroups

"Garry has carefully curated 50 golden rules that are valuable to a wide audience – from aspiring entrepreneurs looking to explore a business idea to seasoned business owners exploring intrapreneurial ideas. The real-world experiences and valuable insights from successful entrepreneurs make the advice provided relevant and practical at the same time."

– Dr Dimitrios Dousios, University of
East Anglia, Business School

"In this must-read book for all entrepreneurs, Garry gives you the tools, framework and mindset to increase your probability of success – I wish I'd had this knowledge when I started."

– Marcus Hemsley, Director and
Co-Founder, Fountain Digital

50
GOLDEN RULES

50 GOLDEN RULES

The Beginner's Guide To Entrepreneurship

Garry Mansell

Foreword by Sahar Hashemi OBE

First published 2023

Copyright © Garry Mansell 2023

The right of Garry Mansell to be identified as the author of this work has been asserted in accordance with the Copyright, Designs & Patents Act 1988.

All rights reserved. No part of this book may be reproduced, stored in a retrieval system, or transmitted in any form or by any means, electronic, electrostatic, magnetic tape, mechanical, photocopying, recording or otherwise, without the written permission of the copyright holder.

Published under licence by Brown Dog Books and The Self-Publishing Partnership Ltd, 10b Greenway Farm, Bath Rd, Wick, nr. Bath BS30 5RL

www.selfpublishingpartnership.co.uk

ISBN printed book: 978-1-83952-667-1
ISBN e-book: 978-1-83952-668-8

Cover design by Kevin Rylands
Internal design by Mac Style

Printed and bound in the UK

This book is printed on FSC® certified paper

This book is dedicated to all entrepreneurs who tried and failed. Without their efforts, dreams and creativity none of us would have learned what works and what doesn't. In their failures, our success was born.

CONTENTS

FOREWORD

When I left Coffee Republic, the company I had started with my brother from my mother's kitchen table, and grew it to 110 stores, someone suggested I write a book about our five-and-a-half-year experience. My initial reaction was resistance, as writing was never my strong point, but I started anyway. My first book draft was around twenty pages long – the shortest book ever written, I thought to myself. I remember giving it to my mother and telling her that was all I had, that was the whole story of starting a coffee bar chain, full stop. In her usual motivating manner, she got me to delve deeper and deeper, to really think about that five-year journey. It took me a while, but I eventually found a pattern in the chaos of our whirlwind journey of turning my personal need for skinny cappuccinos into a 100-strong coffee bar chain. That pattern, I found, was entrepreneurship.

I found that the steps we had taken were not unique in any way. By reading other stories, I learnt that all entrepreneurs essentially make the same journey. There was essentially a method to the madness. The process of turning a fragile bubble of an idea into reality puts everyone on the same course. You use the same behaviours. You use the same toolkit. Which is why I called my first book *Anyone Can Do It*, meaning exactly that, anyone *can* do it. *Anyone* can be an entrepreneur. It's not about a particular personality or skill set.

Entrepreneurship is a process anyone can follow, a step-by-step methodology that takes you from idea to reality. Once you take the leap, you start behaving entrepreneurially, almost automatically.

Many people have the chronology of entrepreneurship backwards in their minds. That's why so many people's great business dreams remain just that – only a dream. No one is born an entrepreneur. You don't need to have exceptional characteristics before you start. You don't need to be an entrepreneur *before* you start. You *become* an entrepreneur during the journey.

It's about behaviour. You become an entrepreneur by actually jumping in and doing it – not talking about it or planning it, and, for sure, not by dreaming about it. What activates and awakens that behaviour is taking the first step and hitting the road. It's on that journey from the fragile bubble of an idea to making it a tangible business that you discover qualities you never even knew you had and become an entrepreneur.

Having said that, while you are on the journey you are going to have a myriad of questions, and you won't know all the answers. And this is where this book of 50 golden rules comes in, filled with Garry's experience and advice, backed up with his real-life anecdotes. I wish there had been a book like this when I was starting, as it would have saved me so many hours and days trying to have coffee with a friend of a friend in some unrelated field who might just know the answer to my burning question – for example, about sales strategies or invoice financing – and they often didn't. So, keep this book by your side and it's like having Garry as your mentor. That means you have everything you need to take that leap – be it starting a business or taking your business to the next level. And my motto in life is "leap and the net will appear". With this book by your side, seems like you're all set.

Sahar Hashemi OBE
London, 14 April 2023
https://www.linkedin.com/in/saharhashemi/

WHO IS THIS BOOK FOR?

Are you an aspiring entrepreneur who's been dreaming of starting your own business? Or have you already taken the plunge and launched your start-up, but are eager to learn more and refine your entrepreneurial skills. If either of these sounds like you, then you've come to the right place. *50 Golden Rules: A Beginner's Guide to Entrepreneurship* is designed to help you navigate the exciting and often unpredictable world of entrepreneurship.

So, who exactly is this book for? I've written this guide with a broad audience in mind:

- The Dreamers: You've got a fantastic business idea that could change the world or, at the very least, your corner of it. You're passionate about your idea but unsure how to make it a reality. This book will help you explore the fundamentals of entrepreneurship, develop a solid business plan and take those crucial first steps towards turning your dreams into a thriving enterprise.
- The Newbies: You've recently started your own business, and it's both thrilling and terrifying. There's so much to learn, and you're hungry for knowledge that will help you avoid common pitfalls and set your business on the path to success. This book will provide practical tips and guidance to help you

navigate the challenges of entrepreneurship and grow your business from the ground up.

- The Curious: Maybe you've been running your own business for a while now, but you're always looking for new ideas and strategies to help you stay ahead of the game. You're curious about what other entrepreneurs have done to succeed and are eager to learn from their experiences. This book will offer valuable insights from a seasoned entrepreneur, giving you fresh ideas and inspiration to apply to your business.
- The Lifelong Learners: As an entrepreneur, you recognise that there's always more to learn, and you're committed to lifelong learning and personal growth. Whether you're an experienced business owner or just starting, this book will provide valuable lessons and best practices from the world of entrepreneurship, helping you become a more effective and well-rounded business leader.

But why should you trust this book? What sets it apart from the countless other entrepreneurship guides on the market?

The answer lies in the approach I have taken. I've distilled the vast and often overwhelming landscape of entrepreneurship into 50 accessible and actionable "golden rules" that cover a wide range of topics, from developing your business idea and building a solid team to mastering marketing strategies and securing funding. These rules are based on real-world experiences and insights from successful entrepreneurs, ensuring that the guidance and advice I provide is practical, relevant and battle-tested.

You'll find engaging anecdotes from my life as a corporate employee, entrepreneur and business advisor throughout the book. The rules I have distilled here cover many topics, but they don't contain get-rich-quick schemes or all the answers. I have aimed to highlight areas for consideration that I know work and that you can follow. I would advise you to consider each for appropriateness to your business, then research and learn from your own further reading. I have even included some suggestions for this alongside some practical guides to help you build a business plan and how to pitch to potential investors. I've tried to bring the concepts to life, making the material informative and enjoyable. I've aimed for a conversational tone that's easy to follow, even if you're brand-new to the world of entrepreneurship.

I aim to make this book feel like a friendly mentor, offering guidance and encouragement to help you succeed in your entrepreneurial journey.

So, whether you're just starting to explore the idea of entrepreneurship, are already knee-deep in the challenges of running your own business, or are simply looking to broaden your knowledge and skills, *50 Golden Rules: A Beginner's Guide to Entrepreneurship* is the perfect companion for your journey.

The wisdom and insights within these pages will inspire, inform and empower you to take your business to new heights, overcome obstacles and achieve the success you've always dreamed of.

Ready to dive in and explore the world of entrepreneurship? Let's get started on this incredible journey together.

WHY I WROTE THIS BOOK

As a successful entrepreneur who's been through the ups and downs of starting and growing a business, I've experienced first-hand the challenges and triumphs of entrepreneurship. Over the years, I've learned countless lessons – some through victories and others through mistakes and setbacks. Throughout my journey, I've often wished I had a comprehensive guide to help me navigate the world of entrepreneurship and avoid common pitfalls.

That's why I decided to write *50 Golden Rules: A Beginner's Guide to Entrepreneurship*. My goal was to create the resource I wish I had when I was starting – a friendly and accessible guide that offers practical advice, real-world guidance and invaluable insights from those who've been there and done that.

Sharing knowledge and experience is crucial to fostering a thriving entrepreneurial community. By pooling our collective wisdom, we can all grow and succeed together. That's why I felt compelled to share the lessons I've learned along the way and the insights I've gleaned from other successful entrepreneurs. This book will serve as a valuable resource and a source of inspiration for readers who are just starting on their entrepreneurial journey or are looking to level up their existing businesses.

50 Golden Rules is more than just a collection of tips and tricks; it reflects my passion for entrepreneurship and commitment to helping others achieve their dreams. I firmly believe anyone can become a successful entrepreneur with the right mindset, determination and access to the right resources. This book is my way of providing that resource and contributing to the entrepreneurial ecosystem.

Throughout the pages of this book, you'll find much practical advice, actionable strategies, and personal anecdotes that paint a vivid picture of what it's like to be an entrepreneur. I've shared some of my own experiences, both the successes and the failures, hoping they will offer readers valuable lessons and insights. By being open and candid about my journey, I want to show you that entrepreneurship can be challenging sailing, but it's a journey worth taking.

My ultimate goal with *50 Golden Rules* is to empower aspiring entrepreneurs to take the leap and pursue their passion, armed with the knowledge and tools they need to succeed. I want to help demystify the world of entrepreneurship and make it accessible to everyone, regardless of their background or experience. By sharing my experience and the experiences of others who have walked this path, I aim to inspire readers to believe in their own potential and take their first steps towards building a successful business.

So, if you're an aspiring entrepreneur, a curious business owner or a lifelong learner, I invite you to join me on this journey. The wisdom and insights shared in this book will prove invaluable as you navigate the exciting and challenging world of entrepreneurship. Together, we can learn, grow and build the businesses of our dreams.

PART I

MINDSET & PERSONAL DEVELOPMENT

Welcome to the Mindset and Personal Development section of *50 Golden Rules: The Beginner's Guide to Entrepreneurship*. In this section, I'll explore some crucial aspects of developing a winning entrepreneurial mindset, including cultivating resilience, embracing failure, mastering time management and building meaningful relationships.

So why not do something different from the start of this book?

Let's start on a negative note.

Your business is probably going to fail. Yes, that's right, you will likely fail.

After all, only about one in twenty businesses that start still exist two years later. It's the reason angel investors know that they are investing in high-risk assets, but they still go ahead and make those investments because they expect that high-risk investments have the potential to generate high rewards as well. If they didn't, they would leave their money in the bank earning less than 5 per cent in interest a year.

Very few entrepreneurs I know have had raging success in their first business.

We all know the stories of entrepreneurs who have walked away from the smoking ruins of previous businesses, leaving upset friends, family, staff and investors behind them.

Many of these entrepreneurs never try again. They seek jobs back in industry and sit there wishing for what could have been. In truth, nothing is wrong with that; I applaud the fact that they tried to deliver their dream and business idea. Sometimes, failure comes simply from being too early. Timing and luck still have a lot to do with business success. My first business was hardly a raging success; it closed through lack of growth and struggled to make a profit. I made some mistakes, but I learned from them, and listened to the excellent advice that was offered to me.

So, as you embark on your entrepreneurial journey, it's essential to develop a growth mindset that empowers you to overcome obstacles, learn from setbacks and make better decisions. The relentless growth mindset is the cornerstone of this mentality, a rule you must embrace wholeheartedly.

Throughout this section, we'll delve into the strategies and approaches you can adopt to cultivate this mindset, including remaining curious, embracing discomfort, developing resilience, practising adaptability and reflecting on your progress.

We'll also explore the importance of embracing failure and learning from mistakes, building resilience and perseverance, mastering time management and prioritisation, and networking and relationship building.

Adopting these golden rules and integrating them into your entrepreneurial journey will unlock new opportunities, drive innovation and ultimately achieve enduring success. So, let's dive in and start cultivating the mindset and personal development skills you need to succeed as an entrepreneur.

CHAPTER 1

CULTIVATING AN ENTREPRENEURIAL MINDSET

"Cultivating a relentless growth mindset is vital for long-term success. This mindset, rooted in continuous personal and professional development, enables you to overcome obstacles, learn from setbacks and make better decisions. To embrace this mentality, stay curious, embrace discomfort, develop resilience, practice adaptability and reflect on your progress. By embodying the relentless growth mindset throughout your entrepreneurial journey, you'll unlock new opportunities, drive innovation and achieve enduring success."

As an aspiring entrepreneur, cultivating an entrepreneurial mindset is crucial to long-term success. The relentless growth mindset is the cornerstone of this mentality, an indispensable rule to embrace on your journey.

The relentless growth mindset is the unyielding pursuit of personal and professional development. It involves continuously challenging yourself, learning from setbacks and adapting to new circumstances. This mindset will empower you to push past obstacles, learn from failures and make better decisions as you progress.

To cultivate a relentless growth mindset, follow these essential steps:

- Remain curious: Always be open to new ideas, perspectives and experiences. Seek out opportunities to learn, whether it's through books, podcasts, courses, or conversations with mentors.
- Embrace discomfort: Accept that growth and comfort cannot coexist. Embrace the pain that comes with learning and pushing your boundaries. It's through this discomfort that you'll discover your true potential.
- Develop resilience: Failure is an inevitable part of entrepreneurship. However, use setbacks as learning experiences and bounce back stronger than before. Strength will help you focus on your goals, regardless of your challenges.
- Practice adaptability: Entrepreneurs must be nimble and ready to pivot in a constantly changing world. Embrace change and adapt your strategies to stay ahead of the competition.
- Reflect and iterate: Regularly evaluate your progress and seek feedback from others. Use this information to refine your approach and make continuous improvements.

Remember, the relentless growth mindset is a lifelong pursuit. As you apply this rule to your entrepreneurial journey, you'll unlock more significant opportunities, foster innovation, and, ultimately, achieve lasting success.

CHAPTER 2

EMBRACING FAILURE AND LEARNING FROM MISTAKES

> *"Cultivate an unwavering belief in your ability to bounce back and view every failure as an opportunity to learn and grow. Practice 'Positive Reframing' by objectively assessing setbacks, extracting valuable lessons and applying them to future endeavours. By harnessing the power of failure, you'll develop resilience, adaptability and a continuous improvement mindset, propelling you towards your ultimate entrepreneurial goals."*

As an entrepreneur, you must cultivate an unwavering belief in your ability to bounce back from setbacks. Embrace that failure and mistakes are part of the journey and a powerful catalyst for personal growth and business success. View every failure as an opportunity to learn, refine and strengthen your entrepreneurial muscles.

To do this, practice the art of "Positive Reframing".

When faced with a setback, resist the urge to dwell on negativity or self-pity.

Instead, assess the situation objectively, extract valuable lessons and apply them to your future endeavours. By harnessing the power of failure, you will develop resilience and adaptability, forging a mindset of continuous improvement that will propel you towards your ultimate entrepreneurial goals.

CHAPTER 3

BUILDING RESILIENCE AND PERSEVERANCE

"When navigating the unpredictable world of entrepreneurship, adopt the practice of 'failing forward' by treating setbacks and challenges as opportunities for growth. Each time you stumble, assess the situation, learn from your mistakes and recalibrate your approach. You'll develop the mental fortitude to turn your entrepreneurial dreams into reality by continuously adapting and thriving on adversity. Remember, every successful entrepreneur has faced setbacks; what sets them apart is their ability to bounce back, learn and forge ahead."

In entrepreneurship, resilience and perseverance are not just desirable traits but essential ingredients for success. As you navigate the unpredictable terrain of building your venture, you will inevitably face setbacks, challenges and failures. The key to developing a winning mindset is to view these experiences not as insurmountable obstacles but as valuable lessons on the path to success.

To build resilience and perseverance, adopt the practice of "failing forward". This means embracing failure as an opportunity for growth and using it to propel you closer to your goals. Each time you stumble, assess what went wrong, learn from your mistakes and recalibrate your approach. This process of continuous adaptation will help you develop the tenacity to overcome future challenges and foster a mindset that thrives on adversity.

Remember that every successful entrepreneur has faced numerous setbacks and failures. Their ability to bounce back, learn and forge ahead is what sets them apart. As you cultivate the art of failing forward, you will find that your resilience and perseverance grow stronger, equipping you with the mental fortitude to turn your entrepreneurial dreams into reality.

CHAPTER 4

TIME MANAGEMENT AND PRIORITISATION

"Use the Power of 3s framework, which involves prioritising, delegating and reflecting. Entrepreneurs should identify the top three daily tasks that align with their goals, learn to delegate tasks to their team and reflect on their daily achievements and challenges. This continuous feedback loop aids in refining time management and decision-making skills, ultimately contributing to a more efficient and successful entrepreneurial journey."

In the realm of entrepreneurship, time is the most valuable currency. Therefore, mastering time management and prioritisation are crucial for personal development and business success. Adopt the Power of 3s framework to streamline your daily activities and enhance your decision-making abilities.

- Prioritise: Begin each day by identifying the top three most important tasks that align with your business goals and personal growth. These tasks should yield the most significant impact and progress towards your objectives. By focusing on these priorities, you will minimise distractions and maximise productivity.

- Delegate: Recognise that you cannot do everything alone as an entrepreneur. Learn to delegate tasks that can be handled by your team, allowing you to concentrate on your top three priorities. Empower your team members to take ownership and develop their skills, fostering a culture of growth and collaboration.
- Reflect: At the end of each day, reflect on your accomplishments, challenges and lessons learned. Evaluate the effectiveness of your prioritisation and delegation strategies and adjust as needed. This continuous feedback loop will help you refine your time management and decision-making skills, leading to a more efficient and successful entrepreneurial journey.

CHAPTER 5

NETWORKING AND RELATIONSHIP BUILDING

> *"Adopt a generous networking mindset, focusing on creating value for others without expecting something in return. Build relationships based on trust and reciprocity, and genuinely invest in others. This approach will deepen your connections, attract opportunities and contribute to your long-term success."*

In entrepreneurship, success is often measured by the strength and depth of your network. Therefore, as you navigate the world of business, adopt a mindset of generosity and genuine connection when building relationships. This rule can be summarised by the mantra: "Give without the expectation of receiving."

When networking, focus on creating value for others first. Offer assistance, share insights and introduce yourself without expecting anything in return. By fostering a giving mentality, you'll create a powerful and positive impression that will, in turn, draw opportunities and connections your way.

Remember, relationships are built on trust and reciprocity. The more you invest in others, the more they invest in you. Approach each interaction with empathy and active listening, showing genuine interest in the person you're engaging with. This will not only deepen your connections but also open doors to unexpected opportunities.

Cultivating a generous networking mindset will set you apart as an entrepreneur and provide a solid foundation for a thriving network rooted in authentic and meaningful relationships. Keep this rule close to heart as you embark on your entrepreneurial journey, and watch as your connections flourish and contribute to your long-term success.

PART II

IDEA GENERATION & VALIDATION

Entrepreneurship is a thrilling journey full of challenges, opportunities and rewards. It requires unique skills, including creativity, resilience, adaptability and a passion for innovation. One of the critical components of entrepreneurial success is the ability to generate and validate business ideas that solve genuine problems and meet customer needs. This process can be complex and time-consuming but also exhilarating and rewarding.

Regarding being rewarded, there is nothing wrong with your reason for building your business being to change your life and lifestyle massively. The odds are you will be employing people. As you do, you will be contributing to helping them build their families, pay their taxes and make a valuable contribution to the society you and they live in.

I will give you one warning though, employing people will be one of the hardest things you do. They are not "resources", they are people, and it is only fitting that, at the end of each month, you will be thinking more about making sure they can pay their mortgages and their bills before you think of your own. One of the skills you will need to get the best from your people is creativity; empathy comes later in the book, and it's that skill that will make you a leader.

This book section focuses on five key areas: identifying market opportunities, evaluating and refining your idea, conducting market research, creating a unique selling proposition, and validating your idea with a minimal viable product.

A small confession is due here from me. I have never done all these things in any of the businesses I have built. Very often, I didn't do my market research and I should have. My idea was so exciting that I didn't even want to think that somebody else may already be doing what I was going to. So if you want to get any form of investment for your business from people other than friends and family, I suggest you don't follow my lead. No investor ever believes an answer from a founder that claims that their business has no competitors.

In conclusion, idea generation and validation are crucial to entrepreneurial success. By following these five golden rules, you can navigate the complexities of the entrepreneurial journey with confidence, creativity and resilience. Whether you're a first-time entrepreneur or a seasoned pro, this section of the book provides valuable insights and practical strategies to help you realise your dreams and make a lasting impact in the world.

CHAPTER 6

IDENTIFYING MARKET OPPORTUNITIES

"Utilise the Triple-S Framework: Scan, Spot and Solve to uncover market opportunities. Conduct thorough market research, identify untapped niches and customer needs, and prototype a solution addressing the problem. This framework will help you navigate the evolving market landscape and position yourself for entrepreneurial success."

To identify market opportunities, adopt the Triple-S Framework, which consists of three key steps: Scan, Spot and Solve. This framework will help you navigate the constantly evolving entrepreneurship landscape and uncover the market's hidden gems.

- Scan: Develop a keen understanding of the market by conducting thorough research on industry trends, emerging technologies and competitor strategies. Stay up to date with news and insights from trusted sources. As you expand your knowledge, keep an open mind and question the status quo.
- Spot: Leverage your market research to recognise untapped niches, pain points and customer needs. Observe consumer behaviour and identify patterns that reveal potential gaps in the market. Then, feel

free to dive deep and explore unconventional ideas; they may hold the key to unique opportunities.

- Solve: Once you've identified a promising opportunity, validate its potential by prototyping a solution that addresses the identified problem or need. Then, engage with your target audience, gather feedback and iterate your solution. Remember, the key to a successful venture is offering a compelling value proposition that distinguishes your offering from competitors.

By embracing the Triple-S Framework, you'll equip yourself with the knowledge and skills to identify and capitalise on market opportunities, positioning yourself for entrepreneurial success.

CHAPTER 7

EVALUATING AND REFINING YOUR IDEA

"Use the '3P' Evaluation Framework – Purpose, Potential and Practicality – to assess your idea. Ensure it has a clear purpose that solves a genuine problem, possesses growth prospects and scalability, and is feasible considering resources, expertise and real-world challenges. This holistic approach sets the foundation for a successful venture and increases the likelihood of long-term entrepreneurial success."

In the entrepreneurship journey, idea generation and validation are crucial to success. When evaluating and refining your idea, consider applying the "3P" Evaluation Framework: Purpose, Potential and Practicality. This framework helps you examine your concept from multiple perspectives, ensuring it's well-rounded and positioned for success.

- Purpose: Analyse the core of your idea and its relevance to the market. Determine if it solves a genuine problem, fulfils a need, or creates a new opportunity. Consider if it aligns with your entrepreneurial values, goals and mission. Your idea must have a clear purpose that resonates with you and your target audience.

- Potential: Assess the growth prospects and scalability of your idea. Research the market size, competitors and target audience. Identify the unique selling points (USPs) distinguishing your idea from the competition. Consider the resources required for growth, possible challenges and how your idea can evolve. Your idea should potentially generate significant revenue and impact the marketplace.
- Practicality: Examine the feasibility of implementing your idea, considering the resources, expertise and timeframe needed for execution. Evaluate the technical aspects, financial requirements and regulatory constraints. Reflect on your skill set and the network of professionals you can collaborate with to bring your idea to life. Considering the real-world limitations and challenges, your vision must be practical and achievable.

In conclusion, when evaluating and refining your idea, the "3P" Evaluation Framework provides a holistic approach, ensuring your concept is purposeful, has potential and is practical. By adhering to this rule, you'll set the foundation for a successful venture and increase the likelihood of long-term entrepreneurial success.

CHAPTER 8

CONDUCTING MARKET RESEARCH

"Follow the 3P Framework for Comprehensive Market Research: Perceive, Probe and Pivot. Understand the market landscape, engage with stakeholders to gather valuable data, and refine your idea based on research findings. Embrace flexibility and adaptability to minimise risks and set your venture up for long-term success."

In the pursuit of entrepreneurial success, conducting thorough market research is an indispensable step. To ensure your idea has a solid foundation and meets the needs of your target audience, adhere to the 3P Framework for Comprehensive Market Research.

- Perceive: Start by developing a deep understanding of the market landscape. Research your competitors, evaluate market trends and identify gaps your product or service can fill. Be aware of emerging technologies and changing customer preferences, as these will play a vital role in shaping the future of your industry.
- Probe: Engage in primary research by interacting with potential customers, industry experts and other stakeholders. Conduct surveys, interviews and

focus groups to gather qualitative and quantitative data. Listen carefully to feedback and opinions and be open to adapting your idea to suit the market's needs better. Analyse the data, looking for patterns and insights that can inform your business strategy.

- Pivot: Using the knowledge gained from your research, refine your idea and adjust your approach as necessary. Be prepared to make critical decisions, such as redefining your target audience, repositioning your product, or even pivoting your business model entirely. Embrace flexibility and adaptability as essential traits of successful entrepreneurs.

Following the 3P Framework for Comprehensive Market Research, you can validate your idea, minimise risks and position your venture for long-term success. Remember, the most successful entrepreneurs are those who are willing to learn, adapt and grow.

CHAPTER 9

CREATING A UNIQUE SELLING PROPOSITION (USP)

"To create a compelling USP, understand your market and competition, identify unmet customer needs and align with your business strengths. Craft a clear, concise message and validate it with your target audience, refining it as necessary. A strong USP will give you a competitive edge and contribute to your entrepreneurial success."

To transform a raw idea into a thriving business, it is vital to identify and communicate your Unique Selling Proposition (USP). A USP sets your offering apart from the competition, demonstrating the distinctive value it brings to your target customers.

- Investigate the landscape: Begin by deeply understanding your target market and competition. Assess the strengths, weaknesses and value propositions of your competitors. This will reveal potential gaps and opportunities for your product or service to make a difference.
- Discover the unmet need: Listen to your customers and identify their unexpressed desires or frustrations. Gather insights from surveys, interviews and focus groups to uncover a latent need that your business can address.

- Align with your strengths: Reflect on your core competencies and resources to ensure your USP is built on a solid foundation. Align your USP with your business's intrinsic strengths, ensuring you can deliver on your promises.
- Craft a concise message: A powerful USP should be clear, concise and easy to understand. Convey your unique value in a single, memorable sentence that captures the essence of your offering and highlights the benefits for your customers.
- Validate and refine: Test your USP with your target audience and gather feedback. Be prepared to iterate and refine your message as you learn more about your customers and their needs.

By crafting a compelling USP that addresses an unmet need, you can secure a competitive edge, attract your ideal customers and pave the way for lasting success in your entrepreneurial journey.

CHAPTER 10

VALIDATING YOUR IDEA WITH MINIMAL VIABLE PRODUCT (MVP)

"Embrace the Lean MVP approach to validate your idea quickly and effectively. Focus on essential features, test with real customers, adapt and iterate based on feedback, and learn from failures. This method maximises chances of success while minimising wasted resources, fostering an agile and adaptive entrepreneurial mindset."

In the world of entrepreneurship, time is your most valuable resource. Never squander it by pursuing an untested idea. The Minimal Viable Product (MVP) approach allows you to validate your concept swiftly and effectively, ensuring that you focus on what truly matters - creating value for your customers.

The Lean MVP methodology involves developing a stripped-down version of your product or service, capturing only the core features needed to address your customers' needs. By rolling out this simplified offering to a small, targeted audience, you gain valuable insights into its viability while minimising risk and resource expenditure.

Remember these fundamental principles when validating your idea with an MVP:

- Focus on the essentials: Identify the core features that solve your customers' problems and prioritise their development. Avoid unnecessary bells and whistles, which can dilute your focus and waste precious resources.
- Test with real customers: Seek feedback from a small, targeted group of potential users. Their input will be invaluable in refining your product and uncovering its true potential.
- Adapt and iterate: Use the feedback from your MVP to make data-driven decisions about your product's direction. Be prepared to pivot or even scrap an idea if it fails to resonate with your target audience.
- Embrace failure as a learning experience: Not every idea will succeed, but each attempt brings new insights and knowledge. Embrace the lessons learned and apply them to future endeavours.

By integrating the Lean MVP approach into your idea validation process, you'll maximise your chances of success while minimising wasted resources. Remember, the entrepreneurial journey is a marathon, not a sprint – always be agile, adaptive and ready to learn from your experiences.

PART III

BUSINESS PLANNING & STRATEGY

As an entrepreneur, crafting a comprehensive business plan is one of the most crucial steps you'll take. It's not just a one-time document, but a living, adapting blueprint that evolves alongside your business. Your business plan should provide a clear direction for your venture, and you should be able to use it as a guide throughout your entrepreneurial journey.

A strong business plan and strategy is something you can refer to over and over; it will keep you on the "straight and narrow" and will make you focus.

One of the most common reasons for business failure is lack of focus and founders chasing the next bright and shiny idea. There is nothing wrong with changing direction or "pivoting", but it must be done in a controlled manner with good reason. Simply claiming that you are applying an agile business model (which I discuss later in the book) is often a founder's poor excuse for not conducting proper research or making informed decisions.

So, when creating your business plan, it's essential to emphasise clarity and conciseness. Clearly articulate your vision, mission and goals, while keeping your plan brief and to the point. This approach will make it easier for both you and potential investors to understand

and evaluate. It is also a great document to share with potential employees to help them understand and buy into your vision. Conduct thorough market research to understand your target market, competition and industry trends. This knowledge will inform your strategies and help you identify opportunities and threats.

I'm a fan of incorporating SMART goals when setting objectives for your business plan. SMART goals are Specific, Measurable, Achievable, Relevant and Time-bound. They provide direction and facilitate progress tracking. You should also develop realistic financial projections, be conservative with your revenue estimates and be generous with your expenses. This approach will help you prepare for unforeseen challenges and remain financially sustainable. I speak as someone who has written his fair share of fanciful business plans with vastly overstated estimates of revenues.

Nowadays, when being asked for funding, investors are cynical when being shown projections of revenues based upon "gaining only 1 per cent of a 1 Billion USD total addressable market (TAM)". They would much rather see real customer or potential customer feedback and a go-to-market plan that reflects a more realistic revenue growth. Trust me, it's much easier to underestimate and over deliver. One of the tests of your business is can it make money and generate positive cash from the real world.

Creating a solid marketing strategy is also critical to the success of your business plan. Define your unique selling proposition (USP) and identify the most effective marketing channels to reach your target audience. Additionally, include an adaptable operational plan outlining your day-to-day operations, including your management structure, staffing requirements and critical processes. Be prepared to adjust as your business evolves.

When creating your business plan, it's crucial to plan for contingencies and foster a culture of continuous improvement. Identify potential risks and develop mitigation strategies. This proactive approach will help you stay agile in the face of challenges. Then, regularly review and update your business plan, keeping it relevant by incorporating new insights, addressing changing market conditions and refining your strategies.

As an entrepreneur, you need a clear direction to navigate the tumultuous waters of the business world. Setting SMART goals is the compass that keeps you on course, providing focus, motivation and a foundation for success. To truly understand your target market, start with a broad scope, then focus on demographics and delve into psychographics. Identify pain points and desires to create a tailored offering, and continuously observe and iterate based on feedback and data.

When analysing your competitors, take a four-step approach to strategic observation. First, identify direct and indirect competitors, research their businesses, benchmark your performance against theirs and adapt and innovate based on insights. By mastering this process, you'll make informed decisions, navigate the competitive landscape and drive your business to success.

When choosing a business model, embracing flexibility in business model design is crucial for long-term success in the ever-changing entrepreneurial landscape. Identify your core value proposition, study competitors, diversify revenue streams, establish a feedback loop and continually refine and iterate your model. By staying adaptable and open to change, you can seize opportunities and maintain relevance in the market.

Remember that your business plan is not set in stone, and it will evolve alongside your business. By treating your business plan as a living document, you'll be better prepared to navigate the complexities of entrepreneurship and lead your venture to success.

CHAPTER 11

CRAFTING A COMPREHENSIVE BUSINESS PLAN

"Treat your business plan as a living, adapting blueprint. Ensure clarity and conciseness, conduct thorough market research, set SMART goals, develop realistic financial projections, create a strong marketing strategy and include adaptable operational plans. Plan for contingencies and foster a culture of continuous improvement, allowing your plan to evolve with your business, ensuring flexibility and adaptability for long-term success."

A comprehensive business plan is the cornerstone of any successful venture.

As you embark on your entrepreneurial journey, remember that a well-crafted business plan is not a one-time document, but a living, adapting blueprint that evolves alongside your business. Embrace the following principles to create a dynamic plan that sets you apart:

- Emphasise clarity and conciseness: Clearly articulate your vision, mission and goals while keeping your plan concise and to-the-point. This will make it easier for you and potential investors to understand and evaluate.

- Conduct thorough market research: Understand your target market, competition and industry trends. This knowledge will inform your strategies and help you identify opportunities and threats.
- Incorporate SMART goals: Set Specific, Measurable, Achievable, Relevant and Time-bound goals. SMART goals provide direction and facilitate progress tracking.
- Develop realistic financial projections: Be conservative with your revenue estimates and generous with your expenses. This approach helps you prepare for unforeseen challenges and remain financially sustainable.
- Create a strong marketing strategy: Define your unique selling proposition (USP) and identify the most effective marketing channels to reach your target audience.
- Include an adaptable operational plan: Outline your day-to-day operations, including your management structure, staffing requirements and critical processes. Be prepared to adjust as your business evolves.
- Plan for contingencies: Identify potential risks and develop mitigation strategies. This proactive approach will help you stay agile in the face of challenges.
- Foster a culture of continuous improvement: Regularly review and update your business plan. Keep it relevant by incorporating new insights, addressing changing market conditions and refining your strategies.

By treating your business plan as a living document, you'll be better prepared to navigate the complexities of entrepreneurship and lead your venture to success. Remember that flexibility and adaptability are essential - they'll serve you well as you grow your business and make your mark on the world.

CHAPTER 12

SETTING SMART GOALS

> *"Set SMART goals to guide your business. Specific, Measurable, Achievable, Relevant and Time-bound objectives provide focus, motivation and direction. Align them with your overall vision and ensure they are realistic and adaptable. By embracing SMART goals within your Business Planning and Strategy, you'll navigate uncertainty, seize opportunities and achieve lasting success."*

As an entrepreneur, you need a clear direction to navigate the tumultuous waters of the business world. Setting SMART goals is the compass that keeps you on course, providing focus, motivation, and a foundation for success. Within Business Planning and Strategy, the importance of SMART goals cannot be overstated.

SMART is an acronym that stands for Specific, Measurable, Achievable, Relevant and Time-bound. Each element plays a crucial role in defining a goal that is both practical and effective:

- Specific: Clearly define your goals and avoid vagueness. A specific goal answers the questions: What do I want to accomplish? Why is this important? Who is involved? Where will this take place?
- Measurable: Quantify your goal to track progress and establish concrete criteria for success. Ask yourself:

How will I know when the goal is achieved? What metrics will I use to measure progress?

- Achievable: Set realistic goals that challenge you but remain attainable. Reflect on the resources, knowledge and time available. Ensure that the goal is possible given these constraints.
- Relevant: Align your goals with your overall business vision and objectives. A relevant goal contributes to the long-term success and growth of your enterprise. Ask: Does this goal make sense within the context of my business? Is it worthwhile?
- Time-bound: Assign a deadline or timeframe to your goals. This creates a sense of urgency and helps prioritise tasks. Establish a clear start and end point while remaining flexible to adapt as circumstances change.

In summary, emphasise the value of setting SMART goals within your Business Planning and Strategy. By crafting a compass that is Specific, Measurable, Achievable, Relevant and Time-bound, you'll empower your business to navigate uncertainty, seize opportunities and achieve lasting success.

CHAPTER 13

DEFINING YOUR TARGET MARKET

"Embrace the Bullseye Approach to target your market effectively. Start broad, then home in on demographics and delve into psychographics. Identify pain points and desires to create a tailored offering. Continuously observe and iterate based on feedback and data. This method will help you deeply understand your target market, driving success with a focused business strategy."

To build a thriving business, you must know your target market like the back of your hand. This clarity enables you to create a compelling value proposition that resonates with your ideal customers. Adopt the Bullseye Approach to define and refine your target market with surgical precision.

Start with a broad scope: Begin by identifying the general industry or sector your product or service fits into. This provides a starting point to narrow down your target market.

- Home in on demographics: Analyse specific demographic factors such as age, gender, income, education and location. These variables will help you identify the group most likely to benefit from your offering.

- Delve into psychographics: To truly understand your target market, explore their interests, values, attitudes and lifestyles. This information will enable you to create tailor-made marketing messages and products that resonate with your ideal customers on a deeper level.
- Identify pain points and desires: Determine the most pressing problems, unmet needs, or desires your target market faces. Then, position your product or service as the solution to these issues, creating an irresistible offering.
- Observe and iterate: Regularly evaluate and adjust your target market definition based on real-world feedback and data. Stay nimble, as market conditions and consumer preferences can change over time.

By following the Bullseye Approach, you'll develop a deep understanding of your target market, empowering you to create a business strategy that hits the mark and drives success.

CHAPTER 14

ANALYSING YOUR COMPETITORS

"Follow a four-step approach to strategic observation: identify direct and indirect competitors, research their businesses, benchmark your performance against theirs and adapt and innovate based on insights. By mastering this process, you'll make informed decisions, navigate the competitive landscape and drive your business to success."

In entrepreneurship, staying ahead in the game demands a keen understanding of your competitors. As you venture into business planning and strategy, never underestimate the importance of analysing your rivals.

To strengthen your market position and ensure a competitive advantage, implement the following four-step approach to the art of strategic observation:

- Identify: Compile a comprehensive list of your direct and indirect competitors. Direct competitors offer similar products or services, while indirect competitors may satisfy the same customer needs through alternative means. Remember, today's ally may be tomorrow's rival.
- Research: Dig deep into your competitors' businesses, examining their products, pricing, target

audience, marketing strategies and unique selling propositions. This will help you identify gaps in the market, capitalise on their weaknesses and foresee potential threats.

- Benchmark: Compare your business performance against your competitors by evaluating key performance indicators (KPIs) such as market share, customer satisfaction and revenue growth. Benchmarking provides a roadmap for improvement and highlights areas where you excel or need to catch up.
- Adapt and innovate: Use the insights gained through research and benchmarking to refine your business strategy. Then, continuously innovate to stay ahead of the curve and create a distinctive value proposition that sets you apart.

By embracing the art of strategic observation, you'll be well-equipped to make informed decisions, navigate the competitive landscape and ultimately propel your business towards success.

CHAPTER 15

CHOOSING A BUSINESS MODEL

"Embracing flexibility in business model design is crucial for long-term success in the ever-changing entrepreneurial landscape. To achieve this, identify your core value proposition, study competitors, diversify revenue streams, establish a feedback loop and continually refine and iterate your model. By staying adaptable and open to change, you can seize opportunities and maintain relevance in the market."

In the dynamic landscape of entrepreneurship, adaptability is critical. When choosing a business model, don't marry yourself to a single, rigid concept. Instead, adopt a flexible and iterative mindset that will allow you to pivot and evolve as the market demands.

When crafting your initial business model, consider the following steps:

- Identify the core value proposition: What unique value does your product or service offer? Ensure this value is clearly defined and communicated in your model.
- Study the competition: Analyse the business models of successful competitors and adapt relevant aspects to suit your venture.

- Diversify revenue streams: Explore multiple sources of income, such as product sales, subscriptions, advertising, or licensing, to minimise dependence on a single revenue stream.
- Establish a feedback loop: Regularly seek input from customers, partners and stakeholders to gauge your business model's effectiveness and identify improvement areas.
- Continually refine and iterate: As market conditions change, so should your business model. Stay attuned to industry trends, customer needs and technological advancements, and be prepared to adjust your strategy accordingly.

Remember, the best business models are those that can adapt to change and remain relevant. By staying flexible and open to new ideas, you'll be well-positioned to seize opportunities and achieve long-term success.

PART IV

LEGAL & FINANCIAL CONSIDERATIONS

Unless you are well versed and very comfortable in this area of your business, then this is a section where I suggest you invest in what the head of legal in one of the businesses I worked in called "the highly paid help". Navigating the legal and financial side of things is sometimes difficult, but it need not be. Trust me, getting this right will make a world of difference for your business.

I sometimes get it wrong, and it has cost me time, money and goodwill. Those of you who know me, one day ask me about taxation in the USA when you are trying to build a business there from the United Kingdom. We have many tax treaties in place that should make these things easier, but they don't seem to.

First, when you're just starting, choosing the proper business structure can be a game-changer. It's not just about what you want now, but also how your business might grow. Think about the legal stuff, taxes and protecting your personal assets. This is where an excellent accountant and law firm can be massive assets to your business and help you. It is not money wasted; it is money well spent.

As you're building your business, you'll be coming up with all sorts of great ideas. A good law firm will help you decide if you must protect those valuable innovations by understanding intellectual property (IP) and trademarks. Registering trademarks and filing for patents can help you keep your competitive edge, while safeguarding trade secrets and copyrights will ensure your unique creations stay safe. But patents take time to get, and they are not global. They can certainly add value to your business when it is sold, but must also be defended. The law can be complex in these areas, but good legal help will guide you wisely.

Regarding patents and copyright infringement you may, if you are in the software business, for example, consider that you need patent infringement insurance. The cost of this is still eye-watering if you want to protect yourself from companies based in the USA suing you for patent infringement. This is sadly, where the patent 'trolls' make their money. Trolls, by the way, claim you are infringing patents they hold, hoping you will settle out of court rather than incur significant legal fees. I faced my share of them and never once paid a claim. In some countries it would appear patents are easy to obtain for ridiculous things, and I do single out the USA in this. Those interested in such things who want to be amused can look at the EFF website for their stupid patent of the month. For example, in 2017 IBM obtained a patent for an "out-of-office email messaging system" which they later "dedicated to the public". I, for one, had been using my email out-of-office notification system for years before that patent was granted.

Now, let's talk about money. To grow your business, you need to have your finances in order. So keep an eye on financial statements, maintain organised records and embrace budgeting. And when it comes to taxes, don't shy away from them - use them to your advantage. Seek professional advice and plan to make the most of tax deductions and credits and there are any number of credits and grants available that professionals can help you keep tabs on and take advantage of.

Finally, always be prepared for the unexpected. Identify potential risks to your business and develop strategies to reduce them. Make sure you're covered with the right insurance and stay informed about industry trends and changes. By fostering a risk-aware culture within your team, you'll ensure your business remains strong in the face of challenges.

Building a successful business starts with a solid legal and financial foundation. Take your time, make smart decisions and don't hesitate to seek professional help when needed.

CHAPTER 16

BUSINESS STRUCTURE AND REGISTRATION

"Choosing the right business structure and registering it wisely is crucial for a successful entrepreneurial journey. To make an informed decision, assess your needs and goals, understand legal implications, weigh tax consequences, protect your personal assets, gauge administrative complexity and register your business with the relevant authorities. Consider seeking professional advice to ensure your venture is built on a solid legal and financial foundation."

As you embark on your entrepreneurial journey, selecting the appropriate business structure for your venture is paramount. This decision can have long-lasting implications on your company's legal, tax and financial landscape. To optimise your business for success, consider the following when determining and registering your business structure:

- Assess your needs and goals: Reflect on your business's vision, objectives and potential growth. Choose a structure that best aligns with these factors and offers flexibility for future adjustments.

- Understand the legal implications: Familiarise yourself with the various business structures (sole proprietorship, partnership, corporation and limited liability company) and the legal responsibilities tied to each. Consider seeking legal advice to help you navigate the complexities.
- Weigh the tax consequences: Each business structure comes with different tax obligations. Consult a tax professional to understand the implications and choose the most tax-efficient structure for your business.
- Protect your personal assets: Consider a business structure limiting your personal liability, such as an LLC or corporation, to safeguard your assets from potential business debts or legal disputes.
- Gauge the administrative complexity: Some structures require more paperwork, regulatory compliance and ongoing administration than others. Ensure you have the resources and commitment to manage these obligations.
- Register your business: Once you've chosen the proper structure, register it with the appropriate government authorities. Keep in mind that the registration process and fees may vary depending on your location and desired business structure.

Remember, the foundation of a successful business starts with a well-thought-out legal and financial framework. Invest time in making an informed decision and seek professional advice when needed to set your venture on a prosperous path.

CHAPTER 17

INTELLECTUAL PROPERTY AND TRADEMARKS

"Safeguarding your innovations is crucial in entrepreneurship. To protect your intellectual property and trademarks, understand the different types of IP, register trademarks, file for patents, protect copyrights, safeguard trade secrets and monitor and enforce your IP rights. Doing so will establish a strong foundation for long-term success and maintain your competitive advantage."

Embarking on an entrepreneurial journey is a thrilling experience full of potential for success, growth and innovation. As you craft your unique products or services, it is essential to protect your intellectual property (IP) and trademarks to maintain a competitive edge and establish your brand identity.

- Understand the different types of IP: IP includes patents, copyrights, trademarks and trade secrets. Familiarise yourself with each type and determine which ones apply to your business. Consult with an IP lawyer, if necessary, to ensure you have a thorough understanding.
- Register trademarks: A trademark represents your brand, including your company's name, logo

and tagline. Register your trademarks with the appropriate government agency to obtain exclusive rights to use and protect them. This will prevent competitors from exploiting your brand identity or causing confusion among your customers.

- File for patents: If your business develops a novel product or technology, consider filing for a patent. A patent grants you exclusive rights to manufacture, sell, or use the invention for a specified period, allowing you to capitalise on your innovation.
- Protect copyrights: Copyrights protect original works of authorship, such as software, written materials, or artistic creations. Register your copyrights to obtain legal protection and to gain leverage in case of infringement.
- Safeguard trade secrets: Keep valuable information, such as formulas, processes, or strategies, confidential. Implement robust security measures, including non-disclosure agreements (NDAs), restricted access to sensitive information, and employee training on the importance of maintaining secrecy.
- Monitor and enforce your IP rights: Regularly monitor the market and competitors to identify potential infringements. If you discover unauthorised use of your IP or trademarks, take prompt legal action to protect your rights and maintain your competitive advantage.

By diligently securing your intellectual property and trademarks, you lay a solid foundation for your business's long-term success, allowing you to focus on what you do best – innovating and delivering exceptional value to your customers.

CHAPTER 18

ACCOUNTING AND FINANCIAL MANAGEMENT

"Mastering your numbers is crucial for entrepreneurs to ensure the long-term success and sustainability of their business. Key aspects include regularly reviewing financial statements, maintaining organised records, embracing budgeting, understanding tax obligations, monitoring cash flow and seeking professional help when needed. By prioritising accurate and timely financial management, entrepreneurs can make informed decisions, minimise risks and maximise profitability for their business."

As an entrepreneur, your financial records are the lifeblood of your business. A successful entrepreneur appreciates the importance of accurate and timely financial management. This crucial aspect of entrepreneurship ensures that you maintain a firm grasp on your company's financial health, enabling you to make informed decisions, minimise risks and maximise profitability.

- Regularly review financial statements: Make it a habit to thoroughly analyse your balance sheet, income statement and cash flow statement. These documents provide insights into your company's financial performance and position, allowing you to identify trends, opportunities and potential issues.

- Keep immaculate records: The importance of well-organised and complete financial records cannot be overstated. Not only do they ensure compliance with tax laws and regulations, but they also serve as a foundation for sound decision-making and strategic planning.
- Embrace budgeting: Prepare a comprehensive budget that outlines expected revenue, expenses and cash flow. Regularly compare your actual performance against the budget to identify areas where you need to make adjustments. Budgeting allows you to allocate resources effectively, control costs and plan for future growth.
- Understand tax obligations: Familiarise yourself with the various tax requirements for your business type and industry. This includes income, sales, payroll and other levies. Consult a tax professional to ensure you're complying with all relevant laws and taking advantage of available deductions and credits.
- Monitor cash flow: Cash is king in any business. Regularly assess your cash flow situation to ensure you have enough funds to cover operational expenses, pay debts and invest in growth. Implement effective cash flow management strategies, such as negotiating favourable payment terms with suppliers, offering early payment incentives to customers and maintaining a cash reserve for emergencies.
- Seek professional help: Don't hesitate to enlist the expertise of a qualified accountant or financial advisor. They can provide valuable guidance on

financial management best practices, tax planning and other critical aspects of running your business.

By prioritising accounting and financial management, you'll be better equipped to navigate entrepreneurship's complex and ever-changing landscape. Remember, a solid financial foundation is the key to sustainable growth and long-term success.

I firmly believe that every business is for sale and has a price. By keeping excellent financial records, when the time comes to sell your business, the questions asked of you by a prospective buyer will be easier to answer if you have kept accurate and timely financial records.

These records are not just for you and the tax authorities; they form the basis of demonstrating to a prospective buyer that your business has been well run and has value. Remember that when you sell your business, the buyer is likely to conduct some form of "due diligence". A large part of this will revolve around the financial aspects of your business. By keeping excellent records, you will be well prepared to answer these questions accurately and rapidly. If you would like to understand what a due diligence process is likely to include for your business, then I would refer you to the last chapter of my first book *Simplify to Succeed*, in which I go into some detail about the topic and how to exit your business.

CHAPTER 19

TAX CONSIDERATIONS AND COMPLIANCE

> *"Embracing taxes as a strategic lever for growth involves staying informed about tax laws, maintaining accurate financial records, leveraging deductions and credits, seeking professional advice and integrating tax planning into your overall business strategy. By doing so, entrepreneurs can optimise their business's financial health, mitigate risks and maintain a competitive edge, ultimately unlocking their venture's full potential."*

As a budding entrepreneur, understanding and managing taxes is vital for your venture's success. Taxes are not just an obligation but also a strategic tool to optimise your business's financial health and growth. Proper tax planning and compliance will enable you to seize opportunities, mitigate risks and maintain a competitive edge.

- Stay informed: Stay up to date on tax laws and regulations, both local and national, as they can change frequently. Knowledge of these laws will help you identify tax-saving opportunities and avoid penalties.

- Recordkeeping is key: Meticulously maintain your financial records to ensure accurate tax filings. This not only keeps you compliant but also helps in tracking your business's financial health and identifying areas of improvement.
- Leverage deductions and credits: As an entrepreneur, you may be eligible for various tax deductions and credits that can reduce your tax liability. Make it a point to explore these opportunities and utilise them to your advantage.
- Seek professional advice: Engage a qualified tax advisor or accountant who can provide expert guidance and ensure your business complies with tax laws. Their experience can help you navigate the complexities of taxation and safeguard your business interests.
- Plan ahead: Tax considerations should be integrated into your overall business strategy. Incorporate tax planning into your financial forecasts and budgeting to optimise cash flow and capitalise on growth opportunities.

Remember, this rule is about more than just complying with tax regulations. By embracing taxes as a strategic lever for growth, you'll build a strong foundation for your entrepreneurial journey and unlock your business's full potential.

CHAPTER 20

RISK MANAGEMENT AND INSURANCE

"Protecting your business with risk management and insurance involves assessing and identifying potential risks, implementing mitigation strategies, obtaining adequate insurance coverage, staying informed and adaptable and fostering a risk-aware culture. By adopting these practices, entrepreneurs can shield their business from uncertainties and ensure its security and longevity in the ever-changing business landscape."

As a budding entrepreneur, you're on a quest to build a business empire and to protect that empire; you need to adopt sound risk management practices and invest in comprehensive insurance coverage. This will be your shield in the uncertain world of business.

- Assess and identify potential risks: Regularly evaluate your business operations, suppliers and partners to identify risks that could disrupt your business. Make sure to conduct comprehensive risk assessments, considering financial, legal and operational aspects, as well as potential natural disasters and public relation crises.

- Implement risk mitigation strategies: Develop and implement proactive strategies to minimise the likelihood and impact of identified risks. This may include diversifying suppliers, implementing safety measures, or adopting stringent quality control processes.
- Insure against the inevitable: Ensure your business has adequate insurance coverage to protect against potential losses. Research and select policies catering to your industry's unique risks and exposures. Common insurance types include general liability, property, business interruption and professional liability.
- Stay informed and adaptable: Regularly review your risk management and insurance strategies to accommodate the ever-changing business landscape. Stay knowledgeable about industry trends, legal changes and emerging risks to make timely adjustments and keep your business fortified.
- Foster a risk-aware culture: Educate your team on the importance of risk management and encourage open communication regarding potential threats. A well-informed and risk-aware team is a valuable asset in maintaining the security and longevity of your business castle.

PART V

MARKETING & SALES

In entrepreneurship, mastering the art of marketing and sales is crucial to your success. It's not enough to have a great product or service, you need to reach and engage your target audience effectively. In this section, we will explore essential concepts and strategies to help you build a powerful brand identity, harness the power of digital marketing and create genuine connections through content marketing and social media.

Additionally, we will delve into the importance of public relations, media outreach and sales techniques to elevate your business in the competitive marketplace.

As an entrepreneur, building a strong brand identity is essential. Your brand is the perception customers have of your business, encompassing your values, vision and unique selling points. Consistency is key, and a cohesive brand identity will help you resonate with your target audience and achieve long-term success. By defining your company's values and vision and maintaining a consistent presence across all marketing channels, you'll establish a powerful brand that stands out.

Digital marketing is an ever-evolving landscape, and harnessing personalisation and data-driven insights is critical for creating impactful strategies. By understanding and segmenting your audience, leveraging data analytics and personalising content, you'll connect with your customers on a deeper level.

Stay agile and continually test, iterate and optimise your digital marketing strategies to ensure their effectiveness and relevance.

Content marketing and social media are valuable tools for cultivating genuine connections and fostering a strong community around your brand. By adhering to the Law of Authentic Engagement, you can create content that stays true to your brand, shares valuable information and encourages two-way communication. Establishing genuine connections with your audience will help your business stand out in the crowded marketplace.

Public relations and media outreach are essential aspects of marketing and sales. Craft engaging, authentic stories that resonate with your target audience to elevate your brand's presence and establish yourself as a thought leader in your industry, allowing you to "punch above your weight". Focus on understanding your audience, creating human-centric narratives and leveraging various channels to maximise your reach.

Finally, sales strategies and techniques play a significant role in boosting your marketing and sales efforts. Embrace the power of storytelling to create emotional connections with your audience, fostering trust and leaving a lasting impression. Understand your audience, humanise your brand, emphasise the benefits and include social proof in your sales narratives.

Master the art of marketing and sales, and watch as your business thrives in the competitive landscape. But recognise that marketing will probably be one of your largest expenditures as a percentage of your expenditure when you first start your business and spend your money wisely.

If you are not a marketer, then employ specialists to help you, but in using them ask them what you can expect as a result and agree the criteria for success. In my opinion, the days are over where entrepreneurs have to accept the careworn phrase that "I know half my marketing budget is wasted; I just don't know which half". Now you can, especially with digital marketing, expect to see just how much every lead has cost you, and you should be able to ask for estimates from your digital marketing agency around the number of leads they expect to generate for your spend.

CHAPTER 21

BUILDING A STRONG BRAND IDENTITY

"Your brand is more than just visuals, it's the perception customers have of your business. Start by defining your values, vision and unique selling points, and use this foundation to create a consistent brand identity across all marketing channels. Remember, building a powerful brand takes time and effort, but with patience and consistency, you'll establish a brand that resonates with your target audience and supports long-term success."

Your brand identity is more than just a logo or a tagline, it's the way your customers and the world perceive your company at large. Building a solid brand identity is crucial to your success as an entrepreneur because it sets the tone for your marketing and sales efforts, and it helps you stand out in a crowded marketplace.

To build a strong brand identity, define your company's values and vision. What do you stand for? What makes your product or service unique? What problem are you solving for your customers? Once you have a clear understanding of these things, you can begin to develop a brand identity that reflects them.

Your brand identity should be consistent across all your marketing and sales channels. This includes your website, social media profiles, print materials and any other channels you use to reach your customers. Use the same colour scheme, fonts and tone of voice to create a cohesive brand identity that is easily recognisable.

Finally, remember that building a strong brand identity takes time and effort. Be patient and stay consistent with your messaging and branding; your efforts will pay off in the long run. Your brand identity will become synonymous with your company's values and vision, and it will help you attract and retain loyal customers who share those same values.

CHAPTER 22

DIGITAL MARKETING STRATEGIES

"Harnessing the power of personalisation and data-driven insights is essential for crafting impactful digital marketing strategies. Start by understanding and segmenting your audience, and leverage data analytics to optimise your campaigns. Personalise content and offers to connect with your customers on a deeper level, and continually test, iterate and optimise your strategies to ensure their relevance and effectiveness. By staying agile and embracing personalisation, you'll elevate your digital marketing game and achieve greater success in connecting with your target audience."

In the digital era, the most successful entrepreneurs recognise the importance of personalisation and data-driven insights in their marketing efforts. To master the art of digital marketing, you must build strategies that resonate with your target audience on a personal level.

- Understand your audience: Dive deep into understanding your target audience's needs, preferences and pain points by conducting surveys, focus groups and analysing customer data. This knowledge will form the foundation of your personalised digital marketing campaigns.

- Segment your audience: Divide your audience into smaller, well-defined segments based on demographics, behaviour, or other factors. This will allow you to create tailored marketing messages and offers that resonate with each group.
- Leverage data analytics: Use data analytics tools to track customer interactions, analyse campaign performance and gather valuable insights. By continuously monitoring and tweaking your digital marketing strategies based on data, you will optimise your return on investment (ROI) and improve overall performance.
- Personalise content and offers: Create customised content and offers that speak directly to your audience's unique needs and preferences. By making your target customers feel valued and understood, you will increase engagement, conversions and brand loyalty.
- Test, iterate and optimise: Continually refine your digital marketing strategies through A/B testing, analysing performance metrics and incorporating feedback from your audience. This process of iteration and optimisation will ensure your campaigns are always fresh, relevant and effective.

Remember, the key to mastering digital marketing is to stay agile, embrace personalisation and use data-driven insights to drive impactful strategies that resonate with your audience.

CHAPTER 23

CONTENT MARKETING AND SOCIAL MEDIA

"The Law of Authentic Engagement is vital for mastering content marketing and social media. Focus on three key principles: staying true to your brand, sharing valuable content and encouraging two-way communication. By following this golden rule, you'll establish genuine connections, foster a strong community and make your business stand out in the crowded marketplace."

In the ever-evolving world of entrepreneurship, mastering the art of content marketing and social media is vital to your success. The Law of Authentic Engagement is a golden rule that guides you through creating a genuine connection with your audience, amplifying your marketing and sales efforts.

To follow this rule, focus on three key principles:

- Be true to your brand: Maintain a consistent and authentic voice across all platforms. Your brand's personality should resonate through every piece of content, showcasing your values and vision. This will create a strong identity your audience can trust and relate to.
- Share valuable content: Deliver content that is both informative and entertaining. Focus on providing

value to your audience through relevant, high-quality material that resonates with their needs and interests. This will foster loyalty, engagement and a strong community around your brand.

- Encourage two-way communication: Social media allows for real-time interaction with your audience. Engage with them by responding to comments, asking questions and encouraging user-generated content. This will show your audience that you care about their opinions and foster a sense of belonging.

By adhering to the Law of Authentic Engagement, you'll create a powerful, relatable brand that thrives on genuine connections, ensuring your business stands out in the crowded marketplace of entrepreneurship.

CHAPTER 24

PUBLIC RELATIONS AND MEDIA OUTREACH

"Craft engaging, authentic stories that resonate with your target audience to elevate your brand's public relations and media outreach efforts. Focus on understanding your audience, human-centric narratives and emotional connections. Keep it simple, showcase your expertise and leverage various channels to maximise your reach. Build strong relationships with media professionals to boost your brand exposure and establish yourself as a thought leader in your industry."

In marketing and sales, one of the most powerful tools at your disposal is the ability to tell captivating stories that resonate with your target audience. As an entrepreneur, you must learn to craft compelling narratives that showcase your brand's unique value proposition, convey your mission and illustrate your journey.

- Be authentic: Embrace your brand's personality and values. Authenticity fosters trust and creates an emotional connection with your audience.
- Know your audience: Understand the demographics, psychographics, and preferences of your target market. This knowledge will enable you to craft stories appealing to their interests and needs.

- Be human-centric: Focus on the people behind your brand, as well as the customers whose lives you're aiming to impact. Share the stories of their challenges, triumphs and dreams.
- Create emotional resonance: Evoke emotions in your storytelling to make your message memorable and relatable. Use vivid language, anecdotes and sensory details to paint a picture in the minds of your audience.
- Keep it simple and concise: In today's fast-paced world, attention spans are shorter than ever. So aim for brevity and clarity, while still delivering your message effectively.
- Demonstrate your expertise: Showcase your industry knowledge and experience by offering valuable insights, tips, or case studies. This will establish you as a thought leader in your field.
- Leverage various channels: Utilise multiple media outlets and platforms (e.g. social media, blogs, podcasts, events) to amplify your message and reach a wider audience.
- Foster relationships with the media: Build strong connections with journalists, influencers and bloggers. This will help you gain more coverage and exposure for your brand.

Remember, your stories are the bridge that connects your brand to the hearts and minds of your audience. So invest in mastering the art of storytelling, and watch as your public relations and media outreach efforts propel your brand to new heights.

CHAPTER 25

SALES STRATEGIES AND TECHNIQUES

"To boost your marketing and sales efforts, harness the power of storytelling. Understand your audience, humanise your brand, emphasise the benefits, use vivid language and include social proof. This approach creates emotional connections, fostering trust and leaving a lasting impression on your target market."

In the realm of marketing and sales, the most successful entrepreneurs have mastered the art of storytelling. By weaving compelling narratives around your products or services, you'll create an emotional connection with your audience, leaving an indelible impression that transcends mere facts and figures.

To harness the power of storytelling in your sales strategy, follow these fundamental principles:

- Understand your audience: Before crafting your story, research your target market to gain insights into their needs, desires and pain points. This will help you create relatable and resonant narratives.
- Humanise your brand: Develop a brand persona that is authentic and approachable. Share stories about your company's origins, values and mission,

showcasing the people behind the products or services.

- Highlight the benefits: Focus on the transformation your product or service brings to customers' lives. Describe the journey from challenge to resolution, emphasising how your offering makes a tangible difference.
- Use vivid language and sensory details: Engage your audience by employing descriptive language that appeals to the senses. Paint a picture in their minds, making your story memorable and immersive.
- Include social proof: Weave customer testimonials and success stories into your narrative. This will not only create trust and credibility but also help potential customers visualise themselves benefiting from your offering.

Remember, stories have the power to captivate, inspire and motivate. By incorporating storytelling into your sales strategies and techniques, you'll create a lasting bond with your audience, setting the stage for sustained entrepreneurial success.

PART VI

PRODUCT DEVELOPMENT & MANAGEMENT

As a budding entrepreneur, you might be eager to bring your innovative ideas to life and create products that resonate with your target audience. This section will equip you with essential insights and practical guidance to navigate the complex and exciting world of product development and management, a cornerstone of any successful business venture.

By highlighting the upcoming rules, I will delve into various aspects of the product development process, from the initial design and prototyping stages to quality assurance and scaling your product. You will recognise the importance of iterative prototyping, feedback loops and embracing an agile mindset throughout the product lifecycle. Moreover, as always, I'll emphasise the role of customer-centricity and the significance of rigorous quality assurance and testing, along with practical tips on effectively managing contractors and outsourcing non-core tasks.

As you progress through this section, keep in mind that a successful product is not only about having a great idea but also about the relentless pursuit of refinement and improvement. It's about being adaptable, responsive to customer feedback and willing to take risks for innovation. By mastering the skills and strategies outlined in this section, you'll be well on your way to turning your entrepreneurial dreams into a reality.

Furthermore, this section will shed light on the crucial role of effective communication and collaboration within your team and with external stakeholders. You'll gain insights about fostering a culture of innovation that encourages creativity and experimentation, while maintaining a strong focus on your product's core value proposition. I will touch on the challenges of scaling your product and explore strategies for managing growth, sustaining momentum and staying ahead of the competition.

Another key aspect I'll address is the need to stay agile and adaptable in an ever-evolving marketplace. You'll discover how to embrace change and pivot your product strategy as needed to remain relevant, competitive and aligned with shifting customer needs and market trends. This adaptability will be instrumental in ensuring your entrepreneurial venture's long-term success and sustainability.

Lastly, we'll discuss the importance of building and nurturing long-lasting relationships with trusted partners, suppliers and contractors. By cultivating a strong network of external resources, you'll be able to scale your business more rapidly, tap into specialised expertise and optimise efficiency as you pursue your entrepreneurial goals.

So, let's dive in and explore the dynamic world of product development and management. Prepare to immerse yourself in an experience that will provide you with invaluable insights and tools to create products that not only meet but exceed your customers' expectations. With these newfound skills and perspectives, you'll be well-equipped to embark on a successful entrepreneurial journey, setting the stage for long-term growth and prosperity.

CHAPTER 26

PRODUCT DESIGN AND DEVELOPMENT PROCESS

"Successful entrepreneurs recognise that the product design and development journey is cyclical and demands continuous adaptation. Encourage creative ideation, generate prototypes and rigorously test them with stakeholders. Analyse feedback, iterate on the design and repeat the process until you achieve optimal results. Embracing this iterative mindset fosters innovation and paves the way to success."

An experienced entrepreneur understands that the path to product perfection is paved with iterations and continuous improvement. In Product Development and Management, the Product Design and Development Process is crucial in ensuring the success of your venture.

As a beginner in entrepreneurship, remember that product design and development is a fluid process, requiring constant feedback and adaptation. Follow these key steps to embrace iterative prototyping and feedback loops:

- Ideate: Encourage your team to brainstorm and generate diverse ideas, combining creativity with a deep understanding of your target market and their needs. Two of the most effective methods of brainstorming I know are mind mapping and brainwriting. Mind mapping is a visual technique that involves creating a central node representing the main problem or idea, and then branching out to related subtopics or sub-ideas. Participants draw lines and connections between these nodes to define relationships and associations. This process helps to organise thoughts, spark new ideas and identify patterns or trends. The other is brainwriting, where participants silently write down their ideas on individual pieces of paper or index cards. The papers are then passed around the group, and each person adds new ideas or builds upon existing ones. This process continues until all participants have contributed to every idea. Brainwriting allows for generating ideas without the pressure of group dynamics or fear of judgment, often resulting in more diverse and creative outcomes.

- Prototype: Convert those ideas into tangible prototypes, whether physical or digital. These initial prototypes don't need to be perfect, they merely serve as a starting point for testing and refining your concept.
- Test: Gather feedback from stakeholders, including customers, team members and experts in the industry. Consider conducting usability tests, focus groups and surveys to get a comprehensive understanding of your product's strengths and weaknesses.
- Analyse: Collect and analyse the test data, identify patterns and trends, and use this information to make informed decisions about your product's design and functionality.

- Iterate: Based on the analysis, revise your prototype and then repeat the testing process. This iterative cycle should continue until your product meets or exceeds your desired performance metrics and customer expectations.
- Launch: Once you have refined your product through iterative prototyping and feedback loops, prepare for a successful launch by ensuring quality control, production and marketing plans are in place.

Remember, the product design and development process is not a linear journey. It's a cyclical, ongoing process that allows you to adapt, learn, and improve. Embracing iterative prototyping and feedback loops will foster innovation and drive your venture towards lasting success.

CHAPTER 27

QUALITY ASSURANCE AND TESTING

> *"Cultivate a culture of quality that involves everyone, from inception to delivery. Be proactive, leveraging user feedback, test-driven development and automation for early detection and resolution of issues. Continuously monitor, optimise and adapt your QA and testing processes to exceed customer expectations and differentiate yourself in the competitive entrepreneurial landscape."*

As an aspiring entrepreneur, never underestimate the importance of a well-designed Quality Assurance (QA) and testing process in product development and management. In business, a product's quality can make or break its success. To ensure consistent and exceptional performance, integrate a comprehensive QA and testing system that permeates every stage of your product lifecycle.

- Implement a culture of quality: Instil the mindset that quality is everyone's responsibility, not just the QA team's. Encourage open communication and collaboration across departments to identify potential issues and improvements.
- Adopt a proactive approach: Implement QA measures early in the development process to identify and fix

potential problems before they escalate. This will save you time, money and resources in the long run.

- Leverage user feedback: Actively seek and incorporate input from your customers and end-users. Their feedback will provide valuable insights into real-world use cases and help identify areas for improvement.
- Utilise test-driven development (TDD): Develop test cases for each feature or functionality before writing the code. This will help you create a more robust product and catch errors early in the development process.
- Automate testing where possible: Automated testing tools can help you execute repetitive tests efficiently, freeing your team to focus on more complex issues. There are many testing tools on the market today, and these include Selenium, JUnit, NUnit, TestNG, Appium and Jenkins. Each tool has its strengths and weaknesses, and the choice of which to use depends on the specific requirements of a project, the development team's expertise and your organisation's resources. It is crucial to thoroughly evaluate different tools to determine which aligns best with your project's needs and constraints.
- Perform thorough regression testing: As you introduce new features and updates, ensure that existing functionalities remain intact and unaffected. This will ensure a seamless user experience. Some of the tools I mentioned above can also help developers conduct regression testing, but two other commercially available tools are also worth a mention here. Ranorex has a user-friendly interface, but I believe only works on Windows platforms at

the moment, and UFT (Unified Functional Testing) is limited to VBScript.

- Continuously monitor and optimise: Regularly review your QA and testing processes to ensure they remain effective and efficient. Implement improvements and new technologies as needed to stay ahead of the curve.

By adopting these principles of rigorous quality assurance and continuous testing, you will create a product that not only meets but exceeds your customers' expectations, earning their loyalty and trust. In the competitive world of entrepreneurship, a commitment to excellence in product development and management will set you apart from the competition and pave the way for long-term success.

CHAPTER 28

SCALING AND ITERATING YOUR PRODUCT

"To excel in product development, adopt an agile mindset, focusing on continuous improvement and customer-centricity. Prioritise testing, learning and refining your product while emphasising core functionality and investing in infrastructure. Stay adaptable and responsive to changing market conditions to achieve long-term entrepreneurial success."

In the realm of product development and management, the process of scaling and iterating your product is crucial for long-term success. As an entrepreneur, it's essential to adopt an agile mindset, which enables you to pivot and adapt as your product evolves. This rule encapsulates the importance of balancing growth and innovation in a rapidly changing market.

To effectively scale and iterate your product, keep these principles in mind:

- Adopt a test-and-learn approach: Embrace the concept of "failing fast" by continuously experimenting, collecting data and refining your product. This iterative process allows you to identify what works and what doesn't, ensuring you always make informed decisions.

- Prioritise customer feedback: Keep your customers at the forefront of your product development process. Actively seek their feedback, listen to their pain points and use their insights to guide your product's evolution. A product that genuinely solves customer problems will naturally scale.
- Focus on core functionality: As you scale, avoid adding unnecessary features that may dilute your product's core value proposition. Instead, prioritise enhancements that streamline user experience and directly address customer needs.
- Invest in infrastructure: Be prepared to invest in the technology, personnel and resources required to support your product's growth. Ensure your infrastructure can handle increased demand and have a plan to scale efficiently as your user base expands.
- Stay agile and adaptable: The market and customer needs will inevitably change. Be prepared to pivot and adjust your product strategy as needed to stay relevant and competitive.

Remember, as you scale and iterate your product, it's crucial to maintain a balance between growth and innovation. By staying agile, responsive to customer feedback and focused on your core value proposition, you'll ensure long-term success in the ever-evolving world of entrepreneurship.

CHAPTER 29

MANAGING YOUR PRODUCT LIFECYCLE

> *"To succeed as an entrepreneur, navigate each stage of your product's lifecycle with agility and foresight. From ideation to exit, continuously iterate, optimise and reinvent to stay relevant and competitive. Cultivate a mindset of adaptability to fuel sustained growth and propel your venture forward."*

In the ever-evolving world of entrepreneurship, adaptability is your most valuable asset. As a successful entrepreneur, you must understand that your product will journey through various stages during its lifecycle, and your ability to manage these transitions will determine the longevity and prosperity of your venture.

- Ideation and Conceptualisation: Begin with a solid foundation by identifying a unique, compelling idea that solves a pressing problem or addresses an unmet need. Engage in thorough market research and customer discovery to validate your concept and ensure it aligns with your target audience's desires.
- Development and Design: Make your idea a tangible product by assembling a skilled team that shares your vision. Embrace agile development methodologies,

incorporating customer feedback and continuous iterations to refine and optimise your product's design and functionality.

- Launch and Market Entry: Execute a comprehensive go-to-market strategy, leveraging digital marketing, public relations and strategic partnerships to drive awareness and adoption of your product. Ensure your supply chain, customer support and sales processes are in place to meet the anticipated demand.
- Growth and Expansion: Continuously monitor and analyse your product's performance, identifying opportunities to scale your business. Consider diversifying your offerings, expanding to new markets and enhancing your product's features and capabilities to maintain a competitive edge.
- Maturity and Reinvention: As market saturation and competition intensify, seek innovative ways to reinvigorate your product and reignite customer interest. Introduce complementary products, explore untapped markets, or pivot your business model to maintain relevancy and drive sustained growth.
- Decline and Exit: Recognise when it's time to move on. If your product has reached the end of its lifecycle, consider sunsetting it gracefully, while focusing on new ventures or leveraging the brand equity and customer base you've built to explore fresh opportunities.

Embracing the art of adaptability throughout your product's lifecycle will empower you to survive and thrive in the ever-changing entrepreneurial landscape. Stay agile, proactive and receptive to change, for that is the true hallmark of a successful entrepreneur.

CHAPTER 30

OUTSOURCING AND MANAGING CONTRACTORS

> *"To effectively capitalise on outsourcing and contractor management, identify non-core tasks, select reliable partners through thorough vetting and establish clear expectations. Prioritise regular communication and cultivate long-lasting relationships with trusted contractors to optimise efficiency, innovation and scalability for enduring entrepreneurial achievement."*

In product development and management, successful entrepreneurs recognise the value of delegating tasks to skilled specialists. Outsourcing and managing contractors amplifies your team's capabilities and creates space for you to focus on your core competencies.

- Identify your needs: Begin by pinpointing the tasks or services that can be outsourced, such as design, manufacturing, or software development. Ensure these are non-core activities that can be effectively managed externally without compromising your business's vision or values.
- Vet your partners: Carefully assess potential partners for expertise, professionalism and reliability. Seek

referrals from your network, evaluate their portfolios and conduct interviews to gauge the compatibility of their work culture with your own.

- Establish clear expectations: Develop well-defined project scopes, timelines and deliverables, outlining specific tasks and responsibilities for each contractor. Clarity breeds success, and a well-structured agreement minimises misunderstandings and streamlines workflow.
- Communicate regularly: Maintain open lines of communication, holding regular check-ins and progress updates to ensure your vision is accurately translated. Encourage feedback and foster an environment where contractors feel comfortable raising concerns and offering insights.
- Build long-term relationships: Invest time and effort in nurturing connections with reliable contractors. A strong network of trusted partners will prove invaluable as your business grows, enabling you to scale rapidly and adapt to changing market demands.

Embrace the power of outsourcing and contractor management to maximise efficiency and innovation. By leveraging external talent, you can focus on your core business, drive growth and achieve entrepreneurial success.

PART VII

OPERATIONS & LOGISTICS

In this section, I'll highlight the vital aspects of operations and logistics that every entrepreneur should be familiar with. From streamlining business processes and mastering supply chain management to excelling in inventory management and building an efficient e-commerce system, I'll help you seek out the essential knowledge and strategies to optimise your business's daily operations.

Operations and logistics form the backbone of any successful business; I know, it was my speciality in Mars, Inc. for some 20 years, ensuring that everything runs smoothly and efficiently. As an entrepreneur, understanding how to optimise these processes will directly impact your business's growth, profitability and long-term sustainability. In this section, you'll gain insights into how to implement continuous improvement, cultivate an adaptive supply chain, manage inventory effectively, create a thriving e-commerce platform and deliver exceptional customer support and service.

I'll begin by discussing the importance of streamlining business processes, where you'll gain knowledge about how to analyse and map workflows, eliminate waste and redundancies, and empower your team to drive operational excellence. Next, we'll explore the intricacies of supply chain management, inventory management and forecasting, providing invaluable insights into building a resilient and agile business that can adapt to the ever-changing market conditions.

E-commerce has become an essential part of modern business. We'll delve into the process of building an efficient e-commerce system that will serve as a powerful platform for your online presence. You'll discover the critical elements of a robust, scalable and user-centric e-commerce infrastructure, as well as how to streamline order processing and leverage data-driven decision-making.

Finally, I'll address the critical aspect of customer support and service, discussing the importance of hiring empathetic, passionate team members and providing them with the right tools and training to deliver exceptional customer experiences. You'll foster loyalty and strengthen your brand by prioritising proactive, customer-centric service.

By the end of this section, you'll have gained invaluable knowledge and insights into the world of operations and logistics, equipping you with the tools and strategies necessary to optimise your business processes and create a sustainable, thriving venture. So, let's dive in and start mastering the art of operations and logistics.

CHAPTER 31

STREAMLINING BUSINESS PROCESSES

"To streamline business processes, relentlessly pursue continuous improvement. Analyse and map processes, eliminate waste and redundancies, optimise and standardise workflows, empower your team, measure performance and stay agile. This approach will foster operational excellence, driving long-term growth and success."

In the dynamic world of entrepreneurship, an unwavering commitment to continuous improvement and optimisation is the key to success. To achieve peak efficiency in your operations and logistics, relentlessly pursue the streamlining of your business processes by embracing the following principles:

- Analyse and map your processes: Begin by documenting each step in your workflows, from start to finish. This will provide you with a clear understanding of the intricacies and dependencies of your business processes, enabling you to identify areas of improvement and potential bottlenecks.
- Eliminate redundancies and waste: Scrutinise each process to find and eliminate non-value-adding activities, duplicated efforts, or time-consuming

tasks. Focus on simplifying and automating wherever possible to reduce waste, save time and boost productivity.

- Optimise and standardise: Create consistent, repeatable processes that facilitate efficiency and minimise errors. Implement best practices and standard operating procedures (SOPs) that are easy to understand and follow, ensuring a uniform approach across your organisation.
- Empower your team: Involve your employees in the process of continuous improvement. Encourage them to contribute ideas, suggestions and feedback. Foster a culture of innovation and learning where everyone is accountable for driving excellence and efficiency.
- Measure and benchmark: Establish clear metrics and key performance indicators (KPIs) for your processes. Regularly track and evaluate performance against these benchmarks, adjusting and refining as necessary to optimise results.
- Stay agile and adaptable: Recognise that change is inevitable and be prepared to adapt your processes as your business grows and evolves continuously. Embrace new technologies, techniques and methodologies that can help you stay ahead of the curve and maintain a competitive edge.

Instilling a mindset of continuous improvement will lay the foundation for operational excellence, setting your venture on the path to long-term growth and success.

CHAPTER 32

SUPPLY CHAIN MANAGEMENT

"To succeed in entrepreneurship, cultivate an adaptive supply chain by fostering strong supplier relationships, investing in technology, diversifying supply sources, maintaining a flexible inventory strategy, establishing contingency plans and prioritising sustainability. This approach ensures your business remains resilient, responsive and poised for growth in a dynamic market."

Adaptability is the key to success in today's fast-paced and ever-evolving world. As an entrepreneur, it is crucial that you understand and continuously refine your supply chain management strategy. An adaptive supply chain not only allows your business to respond swiftly to fluctuations in demand, but also to mitigate risks and seize new opportunities.

To master the art of adaptive supply chain management, follow these guidelines:

- Foster close relationships with suppliers: Building strong partnerships with your suppliers is essential to ensure a smooth flow of goods and services. You can anticipate potential disruptions and collaborate on solutions by working closely with them.

- Invest in technology: Utilise modern supply chain management software and other tools to enhance your visibility, monitor performance and streamline processes. Embrace digitisation to optimise your supply chain.
- Diversify your supply sources: Never rely on a single supplier or location. By diversifying your supply chain, you reduce the risk of disruptions and increase your ability to react to sudden changes in the market.
- Maintain a flexible inventory strategy: Adopt a dynamic inventory management approach that allows you to respond effectively to changes in demand. Regularly re-evaluate your inventory levels and adjust accordingly.
- Establish contingency plans: Develop robust contingency plans to handle potential disruptions in your supply chain. Include backup suppliers, alternative transportation routes and emergency stockpiles in your plans.
- Emphasise sustainability: Prioritise sustainable practices in your supply chain, as they benefit the environment and improve your brand's reputation and long-term resilience.

By implementing these strategies, you will build a robust and flexible supply chain that will serve as the backbone of your business's growth and success. Adaptability in supply chain management is essential to navigating the unpredictable waters of entrepreneurship.

CHAPTER 33

INVENTORY MANAGEMENT AND FORECASTING

"Maximise efficiency and profitability by embracing data analytics to forecast demand accurately, optimising safety stock levels, adopting a just-in-time approach, monitoring inventory turnover and refining forecasting models continuously. Stay agile and adaptable to thrive in the ever-changing world of entrepreneurship."

In the realm of entrepreneurship, a well-oiled supply chain is essential for sustained success. As such, mastering the art of agile inventory management and data-driven forecasting is paramount. This rule will ensure your business thrives while minimising excess stock, wastage and potential losses.

- Embrace data analytics: Harness the power of data to identify patterns and trends in customer behaviour, product demand, and market fluctuations. Utilise cutting-edge tools to refine your forecasting models, and always be ready to adapt to change. There are many software tools on the market today that offer this kind of functionality. Most of the best-known tools, such as Oracle NetSuite and SAP will be beyond the price range and be too functionally rich for new businesses. Some tools are more suited to the start-up, being cloud-based and containing a good level of functionality. I include in this, tools like Zoho Inventory, which integrates with other Zoho offerings and QuickBooks Commerce, that also has good integration capabilities. These are worth considering, but you should also continue to monitor the costs associated with using them since they can become expensive as your use of them grows.

- Establish a safety stock: To mitigate the risks of stock-outs, identify the optimal safety stock level for each product. This buffer ensures you can meet unexpected demand surges and maintain customer satisfaction.
- Adopt a just-in-time approach: Optimise your lead times and minimise inventory holding costs by ordering stock as close as possible to the point of sale. This approach requires meticulous planning and strong supplier relationships, but it can significantly improve cash flow.
- Monitor inventory turnover: Regularly track inventory turnover rates to gauge the efficiency of your operations. A high turnover rate indicates that products are selling well and that your forecasting is accurate, while a low rate might suggest overstocking or outdated merchandise.
- Continuously refine your forecasting models: As your business grows and market conditions change, ensure that your forecasting models evolve to maintain accuracy. Review historical data and incorporate real-time feedback to make informed adjustments.

By adhering to this rule and cultivating an agile, data-driven mindset, you'll set the stage for streamlined operations, reduced overhead costs and sustained profitability in your entrepreneurial journey.

CHAPTER 34

BUILDING AN EFFICIENT E-COMMERCE SYSTEM

> *"Develop a robust, scalable and user-centric e-commerce infrastructure that ensures smooth operations and growth. Focus on reliable platforms, intuitive design, streamlined order processing and data-driven decision-making to create a successful online business."*

In Operations and Logistics, building an efficient e-commerce system is paramount to your business success. To create a thriving online platform that stands the test of time and competition, invest in a robust, scalable and user-centric framework.

- Robust Infrastructure: Choose a reliable and secure e-commerce platform that accommodates your business needs and growth potential. Ensure that it can handle increased traffic and transactions, with an uptime guarantee to minimise disruptions to your online presence. It is possible to start your business by using the e-commerce functions built into your web design application such as Wix and Squarespace. Still, as your business progresses you may want to investigate the use of products such as Shopify and BigCommerce. As your business scales, you may eventually need the power of tools such as Magento.

- Scalable Solutions: Embrace the modularity of your e-commerce system by incorporating easily upgradable components. As your business expands, your system should adapt and grow accordingly, without compromising performance or user experience.
- User-centric Design: Prioritise an intuitive, visually appealing and accessible user interface that caters to a diverse audience. Seamlessly integrate navigation, search and checkout features, while maintaining consistent brand identity across all channels.
- Streamlined Order Processing: Implement an automated and efficient order management system to expedite order fulfilment and minimise errors. Integrate real-time inventory tracking, shipping, and returns management to ensure a seamless customer experience.
- Data-driven Decision-making: Leverage analytics and customer insights to identify trends, optimise performance and enhance user engagement. Use this data to refine your e-commerce strategy, making informed decisions that drive growth and customer satisfaction. Many of the e-commerce platforms on the market today contain functionality that will aid and guide your decision-making in this area, and it should be one of the considerations in your buying decision even in the early days of your business.

Remember, your e-commerce system is the backbone of your online business. By investing in a robust, scalable and user-centric framework, you lay the foundation for a thriving entrepreneurial venture that stands out in the digital landscape.

CHAPTER 35

CUSTOMER SUPPORT AND SERVICE

"Hire empathetic, passionate team members and equip them with the right tools and training. Offer accessible communication channels, embrace customer feedback and track support performance through KPIs. Prioritise proactive, customer-centric service to foster loyalty and strengthen your brand."

In the realm of Operations and Logistics, never underestimate the power of exceptional customer support and service. It can make or break your business, directly influencing customer loyalty and word-of-mouth marketing.

To create a proactive and empathetic customer support culture, follow these guidelines:

- Hire people with a genuine passion for helping others. Empathy, patience and problem-solving abilities are vital qualities to look for in your support team.
- Empower your team with the right tools, resources and training to respond effectively and efficiently to customer concerns. Encourage them to own customer issues and seek continuous improvement. Many software tools are available to help your team

support your clients each with its own strengths and weaknesses. Tools worth considering include Zoho Desk, which offers integration with any other Zoho products you use. ZenDesk is a well-established industry leader that may be expensive for most start-ups to use but is comprehensive. FreshDesk is well-liked and used by several start-up businesses. Help Scout and Intercom are other offerings that are worthy of consideration.

- Make it easy for customers to reach out. Offer multiple communication channels, such as email, phone, chat and social media, and ensure your response time is quick and reliable.
- Foster a feedback-oriented mindset. Encourage customers to share their experiences and listen to their suggestions. This information is invaluable for improving your products, services and support strategies.
- Measure the performance of your customer support team through key performance indicators (KPIs) like customer satisfaction (CSAT), net promoter score (NPS) and first contact resolution (FCR). Use this data to identify areas for improvement and reward top performers.

Remember, every interaction with a customer is an opportunity to strengthen your brand reputation and foster long-term loyalty. By cultivating a proactive and empathetic customer support culture, you will lay the foundation for a successful and sustainable business.

PART VIII

HUMAN RESOURCES & TEAM BUILDING

This section will cover the most difficult aspects of the business you build – the people inside it. If you are serious about being an entrepreneur that builds a successful company, you cannot do it without others, and you must truly embrace the adage that your people are your biggest asset. Do not pay lip service to it.

One of the areas I perhaps get most involved in during my consulting work with start-ups or early-stage growth businesses is company culture. Everybody seems to want, or thinks they have, an excellent company culture, but few founders can easily explain to me what that means.

Indeed, very few realise that even if you provide marvellous working conditions, a great benefits package and even put a brand-new gold coin into a food hamper that you send to every employee at holiday times, you can still have a bad culture in your company. Many founders are surprised when I tell them that the way they behave sets the company culture. For example, if you bully your immediate reports, they will soon start to bully their staff. Your behaviour reflects down the organisation. Changing your behaviour as a founder can often lead to a much-improved company culture; your staff may even start to thank you for that hamper with a gold coin in.

A high-performing team is a crucial component of entrepreneurial success. The synergy, collaboration and shared drive to excel can propel your business to new heights. So as you assemble your dream team, it's essential to focus on several key strategies that will enable your team members to thrive and contribute their best work.

One of the most critical aspects of building a high-performing team is establishing clear roles and responsibilities. Ensure that each team member understands their role, obligations and how their work contributes to the overall goals of the business. This clarity enables employees to focus on their tasks and work effectively towards a shared vision.

Open communication is another vital element of a high-performing team. Encourage an environment where team members feel comfortable sharing ideas, feedback and concerns. Open communication not only leads to better problem-solving and innovation but also builds trust and a sense of camaraderie within the team.

In addition to fostering open communication, it's essential to provide growth opportunities. Support your team's professional and personal development by offering mentorship, skill development programs and career advancement opportunities. This commitment to growth will motivate team members to stay with your company and help them become more effective and valuable contributors to your business.

Nurturing a culture of accountability and recognition is another key ingredient in building a high-performing team. Hold team members accountable for their performance and celebrate big and small successes. Implement a fair system for recognising and rewarding exceptional performance to encourage continued dedication and hard work.

Embrace "Situational leadership", a flexible and adaptive leadership style that emphasises tailoring your approach to suit the specific needs, abilities and circumstances of the individuals or team being led. This leadership model posits that there is no single "best" way to lead; instead, effective leaders must assess the situation, the maturity or competence level of their team members and adapt their leadership style accordingly. In addition, by employing a range of directive and supportive behaviours, situational leaders can foster a dynamic and responsive environment where team members feel empowered, engaged, and supported in achieving their goals.

Lastly, don't forget the importance of fostering a sense of unity and belonging among your team members. Promote teamwork, collaboration and an inclusive environment that values diverse perspectives and experiences. This unity will help your team members feel connected to the business, its goals and each other, ultimately driving your entrepreneurial venture towards success.

By focusing on these strategies, you will create a cohesive, motivated and high-performing team that will serve as the backbone of your business and the driving force behind its success.

CHAPTER 36

HIRING YOUR FIRST EMPLOYEES

"When hiring your first employees, prioritise attitude over skill. Seek dedicated, passionate and adaptable individuals who align with your vision. Skills can be developed, but a positive attitude and strong work ethic are invaluable for fostering a successful and collaborative company culture. Invest in training and developing your team to ensure long-lasting success."

As you embark on the entrepreneurship journey and begin assembling your team, it's crucial to recognise the importance of hiring your first employees. These early hires will set the tone for your company culture and lay the groundwork for future success.

When building your team, prioritise attitude over skill. While technical know-how is important, a passionate, dedicated and coachable employee with the right attitude can be the cornerstone of your success. Test a candidate's "learning agility". When this is high, their ability to learn rapidly will greatly benefit your start-up. Seek out candidates who share your values, vision and passion for the project.

Remember that skills can be developed over time, but a positive attitude and strong work ethic are innate qualities that can't be taught. Instead, surround yourself with employees who are eager to learn, adaptable and resilient. These are the team members who will embrace challenges, grow with your company and contribute to an innovative and collaborative environment.

As a leader, commit to providing the necessary training and resources for your team to succeed. Develop your employees' skills through mentorship, workshops and professional development opportunities. This investment in your people will boost their capabilities and demonstrate your commitment to their growth and success.

When you prioritise attitude in your hiring process, you build a strong foundation for your team, foster a positive company culture and drive long-lasting success for your entrepreneurial venture.

CHAPTER 37

CULTIVATING A POSITIVE COMPANY CULTURE

"Build a thriving business by cultivating a positive company culture centred on trust, empowerment, collaboration, diversity and well-being. Encourage transparent communication, provide growth opportunities, celebrate successes together, embrace diverse perspectives and prioritise work-life balance. This will inspire innovation, boost performance and retain top talent, paving the way for entrepreneurial success."

A thriving company culture is the backbone of a successful business. As an entrepreneur, it is essential to create an environment where employees feel connected, inspired and motivated to bring their best selves to work every day. To cultivate a positive company culture, focus on fostering trust and empowerment within your team.

- Trust your employees: Encourage a culture of transparency, open communication and shared responsibility. Trust your team members to make decisions and own their work, and they will repay you with loyalty and commitment.
- Empower your employees: Offer opportunities for professional growth and skill development. Provide

resources, support and encourage employees to take on new challenges and responsibilities. Recognise their accomplishments and celebrate their success.

- Encourage collaboration and teamwork: Foster a sense of unity by promoting teamwork and open communication. Create opportunities for cross-functional collaboration and knowledge sharing. Celebrate team successes and learn from setbacks together.
- Embrace diversity and inclusion: Create an inclusive work environment that values different perspectives, backgrounds and experiences. Promote a sense of belonging, respect and mutual understanding among team members. Encourage open conversations about diversity and inclusion, and actively work to address any issues that may arise.
- Prioritise well-being and work-life balance: Encourage healthy habits and create policies that support work-life balance. Recognise the importance of mental and physical well-being and provide resources for employees to maintain a healthy lifestyle.

By embedding trust and empowerment in your company culture, you will create a positive work environment that inspires innovation, promotes high performance and retains top talent. As a result, your business will thrive, and you will be well on your way to entrepreneurial success.

CHAPTER 38

EMPLOYEE RETENTION AND MOTIVATION

"Foster employee retention and motivation by establishing a clear mission, promoting a growth mindset, recognising achievements, supporting work-life balance and encouraging open communication. This approach creates a thriving work environment that inspires, values and empowers team members, leading to sustained business success."

In the realm of entrepreneurship, a company's most valuable asset is its people. To build a successful business, it is essential to not only attract top talent but also to retain and motivate them. By cultivating a culture of purpose and growth, you can create an environment where employees are driven to contribute their best work and remain committed to your organisation.

- Establish a clear mission and vision: Communicate the company's core values, long-term goals, and overall purpose to every team member. This shared understanding gives employees a sense of meaning and direction, inspiring them to align their personal aspirations with the organisation's objectives.
- Foster a growth mindset: Encourage continuous learning and development by providing opportunities

for skill enhancement, mentorship and career advancement. This shows your commitment to their personal and professional growth, motivating employees to stay and grow with your organisation.

- Recognise and reward achievements: Celebrate both individual and team successes, acknowledging the hard work and dedication that drive your business forward. Implement a fair and transparent reward system to incentivise exceptional performance and reinforce the value of employee contributions.
- Promote work-life balance: Ensure that employees have the resources and flexibility to maintain a healthy balance between their personal and professional lives. In addition, by demonstrating empathy and understanding, you foster loyalty and commitment from your team members.
- Encourage open communication: Create an atmosphere where employees feel comfortable sharing their ideas, concerns and feedback. This collaborative approach leads to innovation and problem-solving and cultivates a sense of ownership and pride in the organisation's success.

By embracing these principles, you will nurture a thriving workplace culture where employees feel inspired, valued and empowered to excel. In turn, this will lead to higher employee retention, increased motivation and a strong foundation for sustainable business growth.

CHAPTER 39

LEADERSHIP AND MANAGEMENT TECHNIQUES

"Nurture a strong, high-performing team by fostering trust, transparency and empathy. Encourage open communication, share crucial information and demonstrate understanding and support. This creates a culture of loyalty and engagement, vital for entrepreneurial success."

In leadership and management, trust is the cornerstone of a strong team. As an entrepreneur, it is crucial to cultivate an environment where trust, transparency and empathy thrive. This will empower your team to work collaboratively, take risks and deliver exceptional results.

To nurture trust, establish open lines of communication and encourage team members to share their thoughts, ideas and concerns. As a leader, be willing to listen actively and respond with understanding and compassion.

Transparency is crucial to building trust. Share important information and updates with your team, including business objectives, financials and progress towards goals. This demonstrates that you value their contributions and believe in their ability to handle challenges. In turn, they will feel a sense of ownership and commitment to the organisation's success.

Empathy is the ability to understand and share the feelings of others. As an entrepreneur, it is vital to practice empathy by recognising the diverse perspectives, emotions and experiences of your team members. Acknowledge their hard work, celebrate successes and provide support during challenging times.

By fostering trust through transparency and empathy, you will create a culture of loyalty, engagement and high performance – essential ingredients for a successful entrepreneurial journey.

CHAPTER 40

CONFLICT RESOLUTION AND NEGOTIATION

"As an entrepreneur, mastering empathetic listening is key for successful conflict resolution and negotiation. Be present, attentive and genuinely interested in understanding your team members' perspectives. Reflect, clarify and validate their emotions while avoiding interruptions or arguments. Maintain objectivity and focus on finding collaborative solutions to foster a supportive, thriving work environment."

As an entrepreneur, your ability to resolve conflicts and negotiate skilfully is crucial to the long-term success of your venture. In the realm of human resources and team building, the art of empathetic listening stands out as a powerful tool for navigating these delicate situations.

Empathetic listening goes beyond merely hearing what others say. It entails understanding the emotions, thoughts and motivations behind their words. By genuinely connecting with your team members and putting yourself in their shoes, you'll be better equipped to address their concerns and find mutually beneficial solutions.

Here's how to practice empathetic listening in conflict resolution and negotiation:

- Be present and attentive: Give your full attention to the person speaking, making eye contact and avoiding distractions. This shows that you value their perspective and are genuinely interested in what they say.
- Reflect and clarify: Paraphrase what you've heard and ask open-ended questions to ensure you've understood their point of view. This helps you avoid misinterpretations and demonstrates your commitment to understanding their concerns.
- Validate their emotions: Acknowledge and validate the feelings the speaker is experiencing. This helps to establish trust and rapport, showing that you respect their feelings and are not dismissing their concerns.
- Resist the urge to interrupt or argue: Allow the other person to express their thoughts without interruption fully. This gives them the space to feel heard and understood, even if you may not agree with their perspective.
- Remain objective and solutions-focused: Stay focused on the issue and work collaboratively to explore potential solutions. Avoid getting personal or bringing up past grievances, which can derail the conversation and hinder progress.

By mastering empathetic listening, you'll be better prepared to navigate the challenges of conflict resolution and negotiation within your team. In addition, this skill will help you foster a supportive and collaborative environment, allowing your venture to thrive as a result.

The Kilmann conflict management tool, also known as the Thomas-Kilmann Conflict Mode Instrument (TKI), is worthy of consideration. It is a widely used framework designed to help individuals understand and manage conflict effectively.

Developed by Kenneth Thomas and Ralph Kilmann, the tool outlines five distinct conflict management styles – competing, collaborating, compromising, avoiding and accommodating – each representing a different combination of assertiveness and cooperativeness.

The TKI encourages individuals to recognise their preferred style and develop the flexibility to switch between styles as needed based on the unique circumstances of each conflict.

By applying Kilmann's conflict management tool, individuals and organisations can navigate conflicts more efficiently, foster healthier communication, improved relationships and more productive outcomes.

PART IX

GROWTH & SCALING

Welcome to a pivotal section in *50 Golden Rules: A Beginner's Guide to Entrepreneurship*, where we can examine the critical aspects of growth and scaling for your entrepreneurial journey. As a budding entrepreneur, your business's success hinges on its ability to adapt, expand and navigate the ever-changing market landscape. In this section, I will provide valuable insights, strategies and best practices that will pave the way for success in entrepreneurship.

First, let's explore the importance of strategic partnerships and their role in growth and scaling. The rule here emphasises that powerful strategic partnerships can unlock new opportunities, create a competitive edge and foster innovation. By cultivating relationships that offer mutual benefits to both parties, you can propel your business forward and reach new heights. Partnerships very often give you something very hard to achieve alone, access to an experienced larger sales force who can sell your goods or services, but partnerships must be mutual and must be nurtured, otherwise they will simply be arrangements in name only that become an overhead, not a source of new sales for both parties.

In addition to forming strong partnerships, mastering the art of identifying growth opportunities is crucial for entrepreneurial success. In this section, I introduce the "3 Ps" of growth: Probe, Prioritise and Pivot. By following these guidelines, you'll be better equipped to recognise potential expansion areas, capitalise on emerging trends and stay agile in the face of market shifts.

Once you've identified promising growth opportunities, it's time to develop a tailored expansion strategy. The rule here highlights the need to approach expansion with purpose and precision. We'll discuss how to define your objectives, develop a precise expansion strategy and measure your progress to ensure the best possible outcomes.

You may encounter opportunities to merge or acquire other businesses as your business grows. This section provides guidance on how to navigate the complex world of mergers and acquisitions (M&A) strategically. By focusing on synergy, due diligence and communication, as well as remaining agile and adaptive throughout the process, you can unlock new growth opportunities and expand your market reach.

Lastly, let's not forget the exciting world of international expansion. Going global presents unique challenges and opportunities. The importance of embracing cultural intelligence and understanding local customs and business practices must be considered here helping you establish a strong international presence and outperform your competitors.

This section covers the essential aspects of growth and scaling, from forming strategic partnerships and identifying growth opportunities to developing tailored expansion strategies and navigating the complexities of mergers and acquisitions. By following the advice and strategies outlined here, you'll be well on your way to achieving long-term success in entrepreneurship. So, let's embark on this exciting journey and explore the endless possibilities that growth and scaling have to offer.

CHAPTER 41

IDENTIFYING GROWTH OPPORTUNITIES

> *"To identify growth opportunities, entrepreneurs must actively explore new markets and trends, prioritise the most promising options and be prepared to adapt their strategies. This approach ensures they remain agile and well-positioned to capitalise on emerging opportunities, driving business success."*

In the realm of growth and scaling, identifying growth opportunities is crucial for entrepreneurial success. To effectively pinpoint these opportunities, implement the "3 Ps" of growth: Probe, Prioritise and Pivot.

- Probe: Constantly explore new markets, customer segments and emerging trends. Keep a keen eye on your competition and research innovative business models. Never settle for complacency; always be on the lookout for potential expansion areas. Attend industry conferences, network with other entrepreneurs and consult with mentors to gain valuable insights.
- Prioritise: With a wealth of opportunities at your disposal, it's essential to prioritise those with the greatest potential impact. Assess each opportunity

based on market size, profitability, competitive landscape and alignment with your company's core strengths. Then create a growth roadmap that outlines your strategic objectives and timelines, ensuring that you allocate resources and efforts accordingly.

- Pivot: As you execute your growth plan, be prepared to adapt and pivot when necessary. Embrace an agile mindset and remain open to refining your approach based on real-time data and feedback. Learn from failures and capitalise on successes, always keeping your ultimate goals in mind. The ability to pivot effectively is a critical differentiator between successful entrepreneurs and those who fall short.

By incorporating the "3 Ps" of growth into your entrepreneurial journey, you'll be better equipped to identify, seize and capitalise on growth opportunities that propel your business to new heights.

CHAPTER 42

EXPANSION STRATEGIES

"Entrepreneurs should approach expansion with purpose and precision to ensure successful growth and scaling. This involves defining the purpose of expansion, developing a precise expansion strategy, carefully considering the timing and method of expansion and measuring and adjusting efforts as needed. By expanding with purpose and precision, entrepreneurs can minimise risk and maximise success in their growth and scaling efforts while staying true to their business goals, values and customer needs."

Expansion is an exciting phase for any business, but it can also be risky if not executed with the right strategy. To ensure successful growth and scaling, entrepreneurs must approach expansion with purpose and precision.

First, define your purpose for expansion. Is it to reach a new market, increase revenue, or strengthen your brand? Whatever your objective, ensure it aligns with your overall business goals and values.

Next, develop a precise expansion strategy. Research and analyse the new market you wish to enter. Determine the potential demand for your product or service, assess the competition and identify any cultural or regulatory differences that may impact your business.

Once you have a clear purpose and strategy, carefully consider the timing and method of expansion. Will you enter the new market through acquisition, partnership, or organic growth? Will you expand domestically or internationally? Ensure you have the necessary resources and infrastructure to support your expansion.

Finally, measure and adjust your expansion efforts. Continuously track your progress and adjust your strategy as needed. Learn from your successes and failures and use this knowledge to refine your approach for future growth.

By expanding with purpose and precision, you can minimise risk and maximise success in your growth and scaling efforts. Remember to stay true to your business goals and values, and always maintain sight of your customers' needs and wants.

CHAPTER 43

BUILDING STRATEGIC PARTNERSHIPS

> *"Forge powerful strategic partnerships by seeking compatible partners who share your vision and values. Ensure open communication, leverage each other's strengths and adapt as needed. Invest in nurturing relationships to unlock new opportunities, gain a competitive edge and drive business growth."*

In the growth and scaling realm, strategic partnerships' power cannot be underestimated. As you navigate the competitive landscape of entrepreneurship, remember that collaboration is often the key to exponential growth.

To build successful strategic partnerships, focus on cultivating relationships that mutually benefit both parties. Identify the unique strengths and resources that each partner brings to the table and harness these synergies to create win-win situations that propel your business forward.

- Assess Compatibility: Look for partners who share your vision, values and long-term goals. Compatibility is the foundation for a strong, enduring partnership.
- Communicate Clearly: Maintain open and transparent communication channels with your partners. The

clarity in expectations, responsibilities and objectives leads to more effective collaboration.

- Leverage Complementary Strengths: Seek out partnerships that enable you to combine your expertise and resources to tackle new markets, improve products or services, or optimise operations.
- Be Flexible and Adaptive: The world of entrepreneurship is constantly evolving. Be prepared to adjust your partnership strategy and goals as the business landscape changes.
- Invest in Relationships: Strong partnerships are built on trust and mutual understanding. Invest time and effort into nurturing your relationships, and the rewards will follow.

Remember, strategic partnerships can unlock new opportunities, create a competitive edge and foster innovation. Follow this approach and watch your business grow to new heights.

CHAPTER 44

MERGERS AND ACQUISITIONS

> *"Pursue mergers and acquisitions (M&A) to fuel growth by targeting synergistic partners and conducting thorough due diligence. Prepare an integration plan, communicate transparently and stay agile to overcome challenges and unite businesses for long-term success."*

Growth and scaling are essential aspects of any entrepreneurial journey. As you navigate the path of entrepreneurship, you will inevitably come across the opportunity to merge or acquire other businesses. Mergers and acquisitions (M&A) can serve as powerful catalysts for growth, if approached strategically and with foresight.

When considering M&A, keep these guiding principles in mind:

- Synergy is vital: Identify potential partners or acquisition targets that complement your business. Look for businesses with complementary products, services, or target markets that can strengthen your value proposition and create a competitive advantage.
- Due diligence is non-negotiable: Thoroughly research and analyse the target company's financials,

organisational structure, culture and potential legal or regulatory issues. This information is crucial for determining a merger or acquisition's feasibility and potential success.

- Plan for integration: M&A is more than just a financial transaction – it's a union of people, processes and systems. Develop a comprehensive integration plan that outlines how the combined entity will operate and how employees from both organisations will be integrated.
- Communicate effectively: Transparent and open communication is essential throughout the M&A process. Address concerns, share your vision and provide regular updates to employees, customers and stakeholders to maintain trust and minimise uncertainty.
- Remain agile and adaptive: Be prepared to adjust your plans and strategies as you navigate the complexities of M&A. Market conditions, regulatory changes, or unforeseen challenges may require you to pivot, but maintaining a flexible approach will help ensure long-term success.

By mastering the art of strategic M&A, you can unlock new growth opportunities, expand your market reach and propel your business to new heights.

CHAPTER 45

GOING GLOBAL: INTERNATIONAL EXPANSION

"To scale globally, learn local customs and business practices, adapt offerings to match preferences and cultivate cultural intelligence in your team. This strategic advantage helps you navigate global complexities, outperform competitors and establish a strong international presence."

Many countries help new businesses when trying to expand into international markets. Numerous government departments and organisations provide support, expertise, trade missions and introductions to international markets and most of this is offered to businesses at little or no cost. So when looking to expand internationally always seek out the help your government can offer your business.

As you prepare to scale your business globally, understanding and respecting cultural diversity is crucial for fostering strong international relationships and unlocking new opportunities. Become well-versed in the local customs, language and business practices of each target market, and adapt your offerings to cater to your global customers' unique tastes and preferences.

Cultivate cultural intelligence within your team and organisation and leverage it as a strategic advantage to seamlessly navigate the complexities of the global marketplace, enabling you to outperform the competition and solidify your presence in the international arena.

PART X

FINANCING YOUR BUSINESS

As we explore the Financing Your Business section of the book, it's important to remember that your ability to secure funding, manage cash flow and make well-informed financial decisions will form the foundation of your business's success. This section provides valuable insights and guidance on navigating the complex world of entrepreneurship, from bootstrapping and crowdfunding to pitching investors and planning your exit strategy.

One of the most crucial decisions you'll face as an entrepreneur is whether to bootstrap or seek external funding. In this section, I highlight the importance of evaluating your business model, setting clear goals and understanding your risk tolerance to determine the most appropriate financing path. In addition, as your business grows, you'll need to master the art of cash flow management and adapt to changes in your financial strategy.

Crowdfunding and alternative financing methods have become increasingly popular as entrepreneurs seek innovative ways to fund their ventures. I will delve into harnessing the power of these platforms, emphasising the importance of transparency, building strong networks, offering valuable rewards and remaining accountable to your backers. By embracing these methods, you can fuel your entrepreneurial dreams, establish credibility and foster a loyal community.

I also explore the art of pitching to investors and raising capital, focusing on tailoring your pitch to resonate with potential investors' unique interests and goals. To maximise your chances of securing investment, research your potential investors' backgrounds, interests and motivations. Craft a pitch that demonstrates your business's value and growth potential while forging a strong connection. Most of all, tell a story and bring your investors with you in what will be a journey. Seek investors that add more than money to your business, find those with genuine experience and expertise in your sector and treasure them.

Cash flow management and financial projections are critical skills for any entrepreneur. Staying adaptable and regularly updating your financial projections, balancing conservative estimates with realism, is key to successfully navigating the dynamic entrepreneurial landscape. In addition, establishing an emergency fund, closely monitoring cash flow and fostering strong relationships with financial partners are essential for ensuring your business's financial health.

Lastly, I heavily emphasise the importance of exit strategies and succession planning. As a forward-thinking entrepreneur, it's vital to consider various exit options, analyse financial outcomes and choose the best path for your goals. In addition, identifying and nurturing potential leaders is crucial for ensuring seamless transitions, safeguarding your business's financial health and securing its long-term success.

In conclusion, this section on Financing Your Business offers a relatively in-depth look at the critical financial aspects of entrepreneurship. By understanding the various funding options, mastering cash flow management and planning for the future, you'll be well-equipped to face the challenges and seize the opportunities that await you on your entrepreneurial journey. So, let's explore ways to finance your business and achieve your entrepreneurial dreams.

CHAPTER 46

BOOTSTRAPPING VS. EXTERNAL FUNDING

"Determine the right financing path by evaluating your business model, setting clear goals and understanding your risk tolerance. Stay vigilant with cash flow management and remain adaptable to changes in your financial strategy. Mastering bootstrapping and external funding will empower you to drive your venture's success."

As an entrepreneur, one of the most critical decisions you'll make in financing your business is whether to bootstrap or seek external funding. Bootstrapping empowers you to maintain control, while external funding can propel rapid growth. However, to choose the right path, you must first understand your business's growth trajectory and financial needs.

- Evaluate your business model: Assess the scalability and profitability of your venture. For example, high-growth, capital-intensive industries may require external funding, while niche or service-based businesses may thrive through bootstrapping.
- Define your goals: Clearly outline your short-term and long-term objectives. Is your aim to build a lifestyle business or to disrupt an industry? This will help determine the appropriate funding approach.

- Analyse your risk tolerance: Bootstrapping requires personal financial investment, whereas external funding may dilute ownership and impose investor expectations. Gauge your comfort level with these risks and choose accordingly.
- Monitor cash flow: Whether bootstrapping or utilising external funding, maintain a keen eye on cash flow management. Efficiently managing resources can make or break your entrepreneurial journey.
- Remain adaptable: Understand that your financial strategy may change as your business evolves. Be prepared to pivot and reassess your financing approach as needed.

By mastering the art of bootstrapping and external funding, you'll be better equipped to navigate the financial challenges of entrepreneurship, ultimately fuelling the success of your venture.

CHAPTER 47

CROWDFUNDING AND ALTERNATIVE FINANCING

> *"Harness the potential of crowdfunding and alternative financing to access capital and support for your venture. Prioritise transparency, build a strong network, offer valuable rewards and remain accountable to your backers. By doing so, you can fuel your entrepreneurial dreams, establish credibility and foster a loyal community."*

In the ever-evolving landscape of entrepreneurship, traditional funding sources may only sometimes be available or sufficient to bring your innovative ideas to life. This is where the beauty of crowdfunding and alternative financing comes into play, offering a democratic, community-driven approach to raising capital.

Crowdfunding lets you showcase your passion and pitch your business to a global audience. By creating compelling stories, visuals and incentives, you can inspire potential backers to invest in your vision. Remember that your crowdfunding campaign should not only aim to raise funds but also serve as a platform to establish credibility, build a community and validate your product or service.

Alternative financing, on the other hand, offers a variety of innovative funding options. Peer-to-peer lending, microloans and revenue-based financing are just a few examples. Explore these options, and choose the one that aligns best with your business model, stage of development and long-term goals.

When considering crowdfunding or alternative financing, remember these key principles:

- Transparency is paramount: Communicate your goals, timelines and risks to potential backers. Honesty and transparency will help you build trust and credibility with your audience.
- Build a strong network: Leverage your personal and professional relationships to create a solid foundation for your campaign. Word-of-mouth is powerful, and a strong network will increase the chances of your campaign's success.
- Deliver value: Offer tangible rewards or experiences that excite your backers and make them feel part of something special. This will encourage them to spread the word and increase your funding potential.
- Stay accountable: Follow through on your promises and keep your backers informed on your progress. This will reinforce their trust and position you for future fundraising endeavours.

By embracing the power of crowdfunding and alternative financing, you can unlock new opportunities, tap into a global network of supporters and fuel your entrepreneurial dreams. Stay open, adaptable and resourceful – these traits will serve you well as you navigate the exciting world of entrepreneurship.

CHAPTER 48

PITCHING TO INVESTORS AND RAISING CAPITAL

> *"To maximise investment success, research potential investors' backgrounds, interests and motivations. Craft your pitch to resonate with their unique goals and preferences, demonstrating your business's value and growth potential. Forge a strong connection by aligning your venture with their needs, enhancing the likelihood of securing capital."*

In financing your business, pitching to investors and raising capital are pivotal steps in your entrepreneurial journey. To maximise the likelihood of securing investment, it is crucial to understand that investors are not a monolithic group; they have diverse interests, motivations and investment strategies.

When crafting your pitch, make sure to research your potential investors thoroughly. Learn about their past investments, sectors of interest and what drives their decision-making process. Align your pitch with their specific goals and preferences, showcasing how your business proposal meets their unique criteria and resonates with their values.

Demonstrate a clear understanding of how your venture addresses current market gaps or solves pressing problems and articulate the potential for growth and returns on investment. Present solid financial projections while being transparent about risks and challenges to prove that you are a credible and reliable entrepreneur.

Remember, the art of pitching is about creating a connection between your business and the investor. When you tailor your pitch to resonate with your investor's unique interests and goals, you demonstrate a deep understanding of their needs and showcase the value of your partnership, increasing the odds of securing the capital you need to propel your business forward.

CHAPTER 49

MANAGING CASH FLOW AND FINANCIAL PROJECTIONS

"Stay adaptable and regularly update your financial projections, balancing conservative estimates with realism. Establish an emergency fund, closely monitor cash flow and foster strong relationships with financial partners to navigate the dynamic entrepreneurial landscape successfully."

As an entrepreneur, your venture's lifeline is anchored in your ability to manage cash flow and create accurate financial projections. This indispensable skill helps you navigate the dynamic landscape of entrepreneurship while minimising risk and maximising opportunities.

- Embrace flexibility: Understand that your financial projections are living documents that must be updated and refined regularly. Stay agile and adapt to the ever-changing business environment by reviewing and adjusting your forecasts frequently.
- Be conservative yet realistic: When creating financial projections, it's wise to be conservative with your revenue estimates and liberal with your expense assumptions. However, don't lose sight of reality; keep your expectations grounded and achievable.

- Plan for contingencies: Establish an emergency fund to sustain your business through unexpected downturns or unforeseen expenses. The financial buffer will not only provide peace of mind but also give you the freedom to seize new opportunities as they arise.
- Track and analyse cash flow: Regularly monitor your cash inflows and outflows, looking for patterns and trends that may impact your business. Use this information to optimise operations, cut unnecessary expenses and ensure liquidity.
- Foster strong relationships with financial partners: Cultivate positive connections with banks, investors and other financial stakeholders. Open communication and transparency will go a long way in securing their trust and support when you need it most.

Remember, as an entrepreneur, your ability to anticipate and respond to financial fluctuations will be crucial to your long-term success. Master the art of fluid financial forecasting and cash flow management to build a resilient and thriving business.

CHAPTER 50

EXIT STRATEGIES AND SUCCESSION PLANNING

> *"Be prepared for every stage of entrepreneurship by prioritising exit strategies and succession planning. Consider various exit options, analyse financial outcomes and choose the best path for your goals. Identify and nurture potential leaders to ensure seamless transitions, safeguarding your business's financial health and long-term success."*

As a budding entrepreneur, it's essential to be prepared for every stage of your business journey, including its eventual exit or transfer. A well-designed exit strategy ensures your business's and its stakeholders' financial stability, while a succession plan guarantees a seamless leadership transition.

When crafting your exit strategy, consider the various ways in which your entrepreneurial journey might culminate. These can include selling your company to a strategic buyer, conducting an initial public offering (IPO), or merging with another business. As you map out your strategy, analyse the potential financial outcomes of each path, and choose the option that best aligns with your long-term goals.

Succession planning goes hand in hand with exit strategy formulation. As you plan, identify key team members who can assume leadership roles in the event of your departure. Nurture their professional growth by providing opportunities to hone their skills and empower them with the necessary knowledge and resources to lead the company effectively.

In summary, this rule emphasises the importance of having a clear exit strategy and succession plan in place. By preparing for your business's future, you are not only safeguarding its financial health but also ensuring its continued success long after your involvement has ended.

CONCLUSION

EMBRACING THE ENTREPRENEURIAL JOURNEY

51

CULTIVATE RESILIENCE IN THE FACE OF UNCERTAINTY

"Embrace the winding road of entrepreneurship by cultivating resilience and learning from setbacks. Balance your well-being with your professional pursuits to sustain passion and achieve long-term success."

Embracing the entrepreneurial journey is about recognising that the path to success is rarely linear. It is a winding road punctuated by highs and lows, triumphs and setbacks. As you navigate the ever-changing landscape, it is essential to develop a deep well of resilience to draw from in times of uncertainty.

To foster this resilience, accept that failure and setbacks are inevitable. Instead, embrace them as valuable lessons, using them as stepping stones to refine your vision and fine-tune your strategies. Remember, entrepreneurship is an ongoing experimentation, adaptation and growth process. By welcoming challenges and staying open to learning, you will continue to evolve as a business leader and, ultimately, reap the rewards of your perseverance.

In pursuing your goals, remember the importance of maintaining balance. Entrepreneurship is a marathon, not a sprint. Nurture your mind, body and spirit, and invest in your relationships. By taking care of yourself, you will be better equipped to overcome obstacles and sustain your passion for the long haul.

52

CONTINUOUS LEARNING AND ADAPTATION

> *"Cultivate a growth mindset by committing to lifelong learning, questioning assumptions and reflecting on experiences. Embrace experimentation, pivot when needed and stay informed about industry trends to thrive in the ever-evolving entrepreneurial landscape. Success lies in knowledge and adaptability."*

In the ever-evolving entrepreneurship landscape, the ability to learn continuously and adapt swiftly to change is paramount. As an entrepreneur, you must cultivate a growth mindset, consistently seeking opportunities to expand your knowledge, sharpen your skills and embrace new ideas.

To harness the power of continuous learning and adaptation, consider the following steps:

- Develop a thirst for knowledge: Commit to lifelong learning by reading books, attending seminars and consuming content from industry experts. Surround yourself with like-minded individuals who challenge and inspire you to grow.
- Challenge assumptions: Question your beliefs and assumptions regularly to foster critical thinking.

Engage in constructive debates and seek diverse perspectives to expand your world understanding.

- Reflect on your experiences: Transform your experiences into valuable lessons by regularly reviewing your successes, failures and key decisions. Then, analyse the outcomes and identify areas for improvement or new strategies.
- Experiment and iterate: Embrace the entrepreneurial spirit of experimentation by testing new ideas, products, or services. Learn from the results, refine your approach and iterate until you reach your desired outcome.
- Adapt to change: Keep a close eye on industry trends, technological advancements and shifts in consumer behaviour. Then, be prepared to pivot your business model or strategy to stay ahead of the curve and capitalise on emerging opportunities.

By integrating continuous learning and adaptation into your entrepreneurial journey, you'll be better equipped to navigate the unpredictable path to success and ultimately build a thriving, sustainable business. Knowledge is power, and adaptability is the key to unlocking your entrepreneurial potential.

CHAPTER 53

GIVING BACK: SOCIAL RESPONSIBILITY AND PHILANTHROPY

> *"Begin your entrepreneurial journey with philanthropy and social responsibility in mind, aligning your efforts with your values. Engage your team, collaborate with partners, measure your impact and share your story to inspire others. By integrating these principles, you'll create a legacy that goes beyond financial success and contributes to a better world."*

As an entrepreneur, your journey is about more than just creating wealth and achieving success for yourself. It's about leveraging your resources, influence and accomplishments to make a lasting, positive impact on the world around you. Embrace the opportunity to give back through social responsibility and philanthropy as part of your business's core values, fostering a legacy far beyond the bottom line.

- Start early: Don't wait until you've made it big to give back. Incorporate philanthropy and social responsibility into your business model from the beginning, setting the tone for a purpose-driven culture that will grow with your company.

- Align with your values: Identify causes and organisations that resonate with your values and your business's values. This authentic connection will make your philanthropic efforts more meaningful and rewarding for all involved.
- Engage your team: Encourage and empower your employees to participate in giving back initiatives. Foster a culture of empathy and compassion, where employees feel they can contribute to the greater good, both individually and as a team.
- Collaborate with partners: Seek out like-minded businesses, organisations and individuals who share your commitment to social responsibility. Form strategic partnerships to amplify your impact and create mutually beneficial outcomes.
- Measure your impact: Regularly evaluate and assess the effectiveness of your philanthropic efforts. By tracking your social impact, you can refine your approach and make data-driven decisions to maximise your contributions to society.
- Share your story: Use your platform to inspire and educate others about the importance of social responsibility and philanthropy. By sharing your journey, you can encourage fellow entrepreneurs and the wider community to join in the effort to create a better world.

By integrating social responsibility and philanthropy into your entrepreneurial journey, you'll cultivate a legacy that extends beyond financial success, enriching the lives of others and creating a more equitable, compassionate world for future generations.

As we conclude *50 Golden Rules: A Beginner's Guide to Entrepreneurship*, it's time to reflect on our incredible journey together. Throughout this book, we've explored the essential aspects of entrepreneurship, delving into the personal and professional qualities that contribute to a successful venture.

The entrepreneurial path is a challenging one, but it is filled with opportunities for growth, learning and transformation. By embracing the ever-changing landscape and cultivating resilience, adaptability and a growth mindset, you will be better equipped to navigate the challenges and seize the opportunities that lie ahead. Remember, the continuous pursuit of improvement and the willingness to learn from setbacks set successful entrepreneurs apart.

As you embark on your entrepreneurial journey, remember the importance of balance and the impact you can have on the world around you. Maintain harmony in your personal and professional life and strive to make a positive difference through social responsibility and philanthropy. By aligning your business's core values with your personal beliefs and passions, you'll create a legacy far beyond financial success.

I hope this book has been an insightful and inspiring resource for you. The entrepreneurial journey can be daunting but, armed with the knowledge and guidance from these pages, you have the foundation to build a thriving, sustainable business. As you move forward, take the lessons learned here and seek new opportunities for growth, learning and positive impact.

Finally, some readers amongst you will see that I have under-promised and over-delivered. The book promised 50 Golden Rules, you have actually received 53 Golden

Rules. I hope this extra value makes you want to follow me on LinkedIn, buy my next or previous book, or even gift them to friends and colleagues. I wrote these not just to educate and amuse but to make a profit. That can't happen without you helping me achieve it.

At this point, I also want to thank my wife, Margaret. Without her patience and tolerance, this, my second book, would never have come to fruition. She helps me maintain balance in my life and steps up to handle many things that allow me the time to write and advise business founders.

Please do carry on and read the Appendices; they contain a great deal of value and some good reference material and suggestions for further reading and immersion.

Thank you for joining me on this journey through the world of entrepreneurship. I wish you the best of luck and success in your future endeavours. May your entrepreneurial journey be filled with discovery, innovation and the realisation of your dreams.

APPENDICES

APPENDIX A

THE ANATOMY OF A WINNING PITCH DECK FOR ANGEL INVESTORS AND VENTURE CAPITALISTS

As an experienced entrepreneur, I understand the importance of securing funding to fuel the growth of a start-up. A well-structured pitch deck is a key to convincing angel investors and venture capitalists that your venture is worth their investment.

I will outline the essential components of a successful pitch deck and briefly summarise why each element should be included.

- The Problem: Start your pitch deck by clearly stating the problem your business aims to solve. Show investors that there's a significant market need and that your target customers are actively seeking a solution. Demonstrating the severity of the problem helps investors understand the potential impact of your solution.
- The Solution: Once you've established the problem, present your solution. Clearly explain your product or service and how it addresses the identified problem. Highlight the unique features and benefits that set your offering apart from competitors. Your solution

should demonstrate innovation and showcase the value it provides to customers.

- Market Size and Opportunity: Present the size of the addressable market and the specific segment you are targeting. Demonstrating a large and growing market opportunity will pique investors' interest and make your venture more attractive. Be sure to back your claims with reliable data and research.
- Business Model: Explain how your business will generate revenue and profits. Outline your pricing strategy, sales channels and customer acquisition.

APPENDIX B

BUILDING A VALUABLE STRATEGIC PLAN

I cannot emphasise enough the importance of a well-crafted strategic plan for new business founders. It should be brief, but it should be well thought through and complete.

While a business plan outlines your venture's operational and financial aspects, a strategic plan focuses on your company's long-term vision, mission, goals and the actions necessary to achieve those objectives. A strategic plan serves as a roadmap to success, providing clarity, direction and a framework for making informed decisions as your business evolves.

A strategic plan should encompass the following components:

1. Vision Statement: Define your company's long-term aspirations and the impact you wish to create in your industry or community.
2. Mission Statement: Describe the purpose of your business, what you aim to achieve and how you intend to add value for your customers.
3. Core Values: Identify the fundamental principles and beliefs guiding your company's culture, behaviour and decision-making.
4. Strategic Goals: Outline the key objectives your business seeks to achieve over the next 3–5 years,

focusing on areas such as growth, market share, innovation and customer satisfaction.

5. Strategies and Tactics: Detail the specific actions and initiatives required to achieve your strategic goals, including resource allocation, timelines and performance metrics.

I recommend using the SWOT (Strengths, Weaknesses, Opportunities and Threats) analysis method I described earlier to build a robust strategic plan. This approach enables you to evaluate your company's internal and external environment, thereby identifying the areas where you can leverage your strengths or address your weaknesses.

1. Strengths: Assess your company's unique capabilities, resources and competitive advantages. Consider factors such as your team's expertise, proprietary technology, or a strong brand reputation.
2. Weaknesses: Identify the areas where your business may be lacking or vulnerable, including skill gaps, limited financial resources, or inefficient processes.
3. Opportunities: Evaluate potential market trends, customer needs, or industry shifts your business can capitalise on to drive growth, innovation, or competitive advantage.
4. Threats: Recognise external factors that may pose risks to your business, such as increased competition, regulatory changes, or economic downturns.

By conducting a comprehensive SWOT analysis, you can develop a well-informed strategic plan that maximises your company's potential while minimising risks.

Remember, a strategic plan is a living document, so revisit and revise it regularly to ensure it remains aligned with your evolving business landscape.

A strategic plan is invaluable for new business founders as it provides a clear vision, direction and framework for success. By integrating SWOT analysis into your planning process, you can build a solid foundation for your entrepreneurial journey and ultimately bring your company's aspirations to fruition. A well-crafted strategic plan also has another benefit. When examining your business and deciding if you need to change things, or even pivot, always refer to your strategic plan. It will not only help you decide what to do, it can also be used to control your impatience and will indicate to you what you should not do.

APPENDIX C

CRAFTING A COMPREHENSIVE BUSINESS PLAN – ESSENTIAL ELEMENTS FOR SUCCESS

As an experienced entrepreneur, I have learned that a well-crafted business plan is crucial for the long-term success of any venture. It serves as a roadmap, guiding your business through its growth and development. In this section, I will outline the essential components of a professional business plan and briefly summarise why each element should be included.

Executive Summary

The executive summary is the first section of your business plan, providing an overview of your entire proposal. It should be concise and compelling, summarising your plan's key points and highlighting your venture's unique aspects. This section is critical because it sets the tone for the rest of the document and encourages readers to explore further.

Company Description

The company description offers a detailed overview of your business, including its mission, vision and goals. It should also outline the company's legal structure and ownership and any significant achievements or milestones. This section establishes your business's identity and demonstrates its long-term potential.

Market Analysis

In the market analysis section, thoroughly examine your industry, target market and competition. This research should include trends, growth projections, customer demographics, and competitor strengths and weaknesses. The market analysis helps investors understand the market landscape and the opportunities your business is poised to seize.

Products and Services

Describe your business's products and services, focusing on their unique features and benefits. Then, explain how they address the needs of your target market and differentiate your company from competitors. This section is crucial for showcasing the value your business provides and justifying its place in the market.

Marketing and Sales Strategy

Outline your marketing and sales strategies, detailing how you plan to attract and retain customers. This section should cover your unique selling proposition (USP), target audience, pricing, distribution channels and promotional efforts. A comprehensive marketing and sales strategy demonstrates your understanding of the market and your ability to reach your target customers.

Operations and Management

Detail your business's day-to-day operations, including your management structure, staffing requirements, key processes and facilities. This section should also address any intellectual property, technology, or equipment necessary for your operations. A well-organised operations and management plan shows investors your business is prepared for efficient and effective execution.

Financial Projections

Provide realistic financial projections, including income statements, balance sheets and cash flow statements for at least three years. These projections should be based on solid research and conservative assumptions, illustrating the financial potential of your business. Financial forecasts are essential for demonstrating the viability and sustainability of your venture to investors.

Appendix (Optional)

An appendix can include any additional information, documentation, or supporting materials useful to readers, such as resumes, patents, licenses, or contracts. Including an appendix can strengthen your business plan by providing additional evidence of your company's capabilities and potential.

In conclusion, a professional business plan should contain these essential components to ensure a comprehensive and well-structured document. By including these elements, you'll create a strong foundation for your venture and increase the likelihood of securing funding and achieving long-term success.

APPENDIX D

SOME COMMON BUSINESS MODELS EMPLOYED BY ENTREPRENEURS

- Product or Service Sales: This business model involves selling physical products or providing services to customers. Entrepreneurs can create and sell unique products or services, or act as retailers, distributors, or resellers of existing products. Retail stores, e-commerce websites and service-based businesses such as consulting, cleaning, or professional services commonly use this model.
- Subscription Model: In this model, customers pay a recurring fee, usually on a monthly or annual basis, to access a product or service. This model is popular with businesses that provide digital products, software as a service (SaaS), content platforms and subscription boxes. The subscription model offers predictable revenue streams and encourages customer retention.
- Freemium Model: This model offers a basic version of a product or service for free while charging for premium features, functionality, or content. It is commonly used by SaaS companies, mobile apps and content platforms. The freemium model aims to acquire a large user base and convert some to paying customers.

- Advertising Model: This model relies on generating revenue through ads placed on a platform, website, or app. Entrepreneurs create content or a platform that attracts users, and advertisers pay to display their ads. This model is used by social media platforms, online publishers and free mobile apps.
- Affiliate Marketing: In this model, entrepreneurs promote and sell products or services of other companies in exchange for a commission on each sale. This model is popular among bloggers, influencers and content creators. It provides a passive income source without needing to create, manufacture, or provide customer support for the products or services sold.
- Licensing Model: Entrepreneurs with proprietary technology, software, or intellectual property can license their assets to other companies for royalties or fees. This model is used by inventors, software developers and creative professionals. Licensing can provide a passive income source and help scale a business without significant investment in manufacturing or distribution.
- Franchising Model: In this model, entrepreneurs sell the rights to use their business model, brand and system to franchisees who operate their own independent locations. Franchise fees and ongoing royalties provide the franchisor with a steady revenue stream. Fast-food restaurants, retail stores and service-based businesses commonly use this model.
- Marketplace Model: This model involves creating a platform that connects buyers, sellers, service providers and customers and takes a commission or fee for each transaction. Examples include

e-commerce marketplaces, gig economy platforms and online service booking platforms. The marketplace model leverages the network effect to scale rapidly and benefit from increased user numbers.

APPENDIX E

SOME COMMON MANAGEMENT TOOLS AND MODELS USED BY ENTREPRENEURS

Lean Start-up: A Detailed Overview

Purpose: The Lean Start-up model is designed to help entrepreneurs rapidly iterate and adapt to market demands by developing a Minimum Viable Product (MVP), measuring its performance and learning from customer feedback. This iterative approach allows start-ups to validate their business ideas, refine their product offerings and pivot when necessary, ultimately saving time and resources by focusing on what customers truly want.

First used by: Eric Ries, who popularised the concept in his book *The Lean Startup*, published in 2011.

Practical aspects:

1. Build: In the first stage, entrepreneurs create a Minimum Viable Product (MVP), which is a basic version of the product or service that incorporates the core features necessary to test its viability in the market. The goal is to launch the MVP quickly and cost-effectively, allowing for faster market testing and feedback.
2. Measure: Once the MVP is launched, entrepreneurs gather data on its performance through various

metrics, such as user engagement, customer acquisition and revenue generation. This data-driven approach helps start-ups make informed decisions about the product's future development and direction.
3. Learn: Entrepreneurs use the data collected during the measure phase to validate their assumptions, learn from customer feedback and determine if the product meets the target market's needs. If the data indicates that the product is not resonating with customers, entrepreneurs may choose to pivot or make changes to the product based on the feedback received.

Real-world examples:

1. Dropbox: The cloud storage company used the Lean Start-up approach to validate their product's market fit. They started by creating a simple video demo to showcase the product's core functionality and gauge customer interest. The overwhelmingly positive response led them to develop an MVP, which was iterated upon based on customer feedback and eventually evolved into the successful product it is today.
2. Zappos: The online shoe retailer Zappos employed the Lean Start-up methodology to test its unique value proposition: offering free shipping and returns on shoes. The company's founder, Nick Swinmurn, launched an MVP by taking pictures of shoes in a local store and posting them online. When customers ordered the shoes, he would buy them from the store and ship them out. This allowed Zappos to validate its business model without investing in inventory and infrastructure upfront.

3. Airbnb: The home-sharing platform began as a simple website allowing the founders to rent air mattresses in their apartment during a conference. This MVP allowed them to test the market's appetite for a peer-to-peer accommodation service. Based on customer feedback, the founders iterated on the concept and expanded it into the global platform we know today.

The Lean Start-up methodology is an excellent framework for entrepreneurs looking to test their business ideas and optimise their product development process. By focusing on rapid iteration, data-driven decision-making and customer feedback, entrepreneurs can build successful businesses that genuinely meet the needs of their target market.

Business Model Canvas: A Detailed Overview

Purpose: The Business Model Canvas is a visual tool designed to help entrepreneurs design, understand and test their business models by outlining nine key building blocks. It provides a structured approach to brainstorming, analysing and refining a business model, making it easier for entrepreneurs to identify potential opportunities and challenges.

First used by: Alexander Osterwalder and Yves Pigneur, who introduced the concept in their 2010 book *Business Model Generation*.

Practical aspects: The Business Model Canvas consists of nine interconnected components that provide a holistic view of a business:

1. Value Proposition: This element defines the unique offering that a business provides to its customers,

detailing the problem it solves, the needs it fulfils, or the benefits it delivers.

2. Customer Segments: This section identifies the specific groups of customers the business aims to serve based on demographics, preferences, needs, or other criteria.
3. Channels: This component outlines the various means by which a business reaches its customers, such as direct sales, retail outlets, or online platforms.
4. Customer Relationships: This element describes the type of relationship a business maintains with its customers, ranging from personalised service to automated interactions.
5. Revenue Streams: This section specifies how a business generates income from its value proposition, including sales, subscriptions, or licensing fees.
6. Key Resources: This component identifies the assets required to deliver the value proposition, such as physical, intellectual, human, or financial resources.
7. Key Activities: This element outlines the primary activities a business must perform to deliver its value proposition, such as production, marketing, or customer support.
8. Key Partnerships: This section describes the relationships with external entities that help a business achieve its goals, including suppliers, distributors, or strategic alliances.
9. Cost Structure: This component details the significant costs incurred by a business while operating, such as fixed costs, variable costs, or economies of scale.

Real-world examples:

1. Spotify: The music streaming service Spotify used the Business Model Canvas to identify and refine its value proposition, focusing on providing a vast music library with personalised recommendations. They also mapped out their customer segments, revenue streams (ad-supported and subscription-based) and key partnerships with music labels and artists.
2. Uber: Uber leveraged the Business Model Canvas to develop its innovative ride-sharing platform. By identifying the value proposition of convenient, on-demand transportation, and mapping out their customer segments, revenue streams and critical resources (such as the driver network and technology platform), Uber was able to create a disruptive business model in the transportation industry.
3. Nespresso: The coffee brand used the Business Model Canvas to develop its unique offering of premium coffee machines and single-serve coffee pods. By outlining their customer segments, value proposition and key partnerships with machine manufacturers and coffee suppliers, Nespresso created a successful and scalable business model.

The Business Model Canvas is a powerful tool for entrepreneurs looking to design, evaluate and refine their business models. By breaking down the complexities of a business into nine key components, the canvas offers a structured approach to brainstorming and analysis that can help entrepreneurs identify potential opportunities, challenges and areas for improvement.

SWOT Analysis: A Detailed Overview

Purpose: The SWOT analysis is a strategic planning tool that helps businesses identify their strengths, weaknesses, opportunities and threats. By analysing these four aspects, entrepreneurs can gain valuable insights into their competitive position, allowing them to make better-informed decisions and develop strategies to capitalise on opportunities and mitigate risks.

First used by: Albert S Humphrey, who developed the concept in the 1960s.

Practical aspects: Entrepreneurs and advisors use a 2x2 matrix to evaluate internal factors (strengths and weaknesses) and external factors (opportunities and threats). The matrix is divided into four quadrants:

1. Strengths: These are the internal attributes, resources, or capabilities that give a business a competitive advantage. Examples include a strong brand, proprietary technology, or a highly skilled workforce.
2. Weaknesses: These are the internal factors that hinder a business's performance or put it at a disadvantage compared to competitors. Examples include limited financial resources, outdated technology, or poor management.
3. Opportunities: These are external factors or trends a business can capitalise on to improve its position or achieve growth. Examples include emerging markets, technological advancements, or changes in consumer preferences.
4. Threats: These are external factors or trends that could negatively impact a business's performance or pose challenges to its survival. Examples include economic downturns, increased competition, or new regulations.

Real-world examples:

1. Apple: In the early 2000s, Apple conducted a SWOT analysis that revealed its strengths in design and innovation, but also identified weaknesses in its limited product range and market share. The company used this analysis to capitalise on the opportunities presented by digital music (launching the iPod and iTunes) and eventually expanding into other markets like smartphones (with the iPhone) and tablets (with the iPad), transforming the company into a global technology leader.
2. Starbucks: Starbucks used a SWOT analysis to evaluate its position in the highly competitive coffee industry. The analysis revealed strengths such as a strong brand, premium product offerings and a global store network, but also identified weaknesses like high prices and limited food options. Starbucks capitalised on opportunities like mobile ordering and expanding its food menu while addressing threats like increased competition from fast-food chains by focusing on customer experience and sustainability initiatives.
3. Tesla: Tesla, the electric vehicle manufacturer, conducted a SWOT analysis to assess its position in the automotive industry. The analysis highlighted technological, innovation and environmental sustainability strengths, but pointed out weaknesses in production capacity and high costs. Tesla focused on opportunities such as expanding its product line-up and building a global charging infrastructure, while addressing threats like competition and regulatory challenges through continuous innovation and strategic partnerships.

The SWOT analysis is a valuable tool for entrepreneurs looking to understand their business's competitive position better and identify areas for growth and improvement. By systematically examining strengths, weaknesses, opportunities and threats, business owners can make well-informed decisions and develop strategies to maximise success in their chosen market.

Objectives and Key Results: A Detailed Overview

Purpose: The Objectives and Key Results (OKR) framework is a goal-setting methodology that helps organisations set, communicate and measure objectives and their outcomes. By using OKRs, businesses can promote focus, alignment and commitment to results, ensuring that everyone in the organisation works towards the same goals.

First used by: Andy Grove at Intel, the OKR framework was later popularised by venture capitalist John Doerr, who introduced it to several successful technology companies, including Google.

Practical aspects: The OKR framework involves two primary components:

1. Objectives: These are high-level, qualitative goals that the organisation aims to achieve. Objectives should be ambitious, inspiring and aligned with the company's mission and vision.
2. Key Results: These are specific, measurable outcomes tied to each objective. Key results should be quantifiable, time-bound, and challenging but achievable. They serve as indicators of progress towards the objectives.

The OKR process typically follows these steps:

1. Set OKRs: At the beginning of a planning period (usually quarterly or annually), entrepreneurs and their teams establish objectives and corresponding key results.
2. Communicate OKRs: Objectives and key results are shared across the organisation, promoting transparency and alignment among team members.
3. Monitor progress: Throughout the planning period, progress towards key results is regularly monitored and discussed, allowing for adjustments and realignment as needed.
4. Review and reflect: At the end of the planning period, teams review their performance, analyse the results and reflect on lessons learned to inform the next round of OKRs.

Real-world examples:

1. Google: Google adopted the OKR framework in its early stages and has credited it as a key factor in its growth and success. The framework has been used across all levels of the organisation, from individual contributors to top executives, helping to align and focus the company's efforts on achieving its ambitious goals.
2. LinkedIn: LinkedIn implemented OKRs to streamline its goal-setting process and align the entire organisation around its mission. The company has utilised OKRs to drive improvements in user experience, customer satisfaction and overall business performance.

3. Adobe: Adobe adopted the OKR framework to foster a culture of innovation and accountability. The company uses OKRs to focus on key priorities, measure progress and drive alignment across teams and departments.

The OKR framework is an effective and proven tool for entrepreneurs and organisations looking to improve goal setting, alignment and performance measurement. By adopting OKRs, businesses can ensure that their teams work towards the same objectives, promoting a culture of focus, accountability and results-driven success.

Blue Ocean Strategy: A Detailed Overview

Purpose: The Blue Ocean Strategy is a business model that helps entrepreneurs create new market spaces and uncontested opportunities by focusing on innovation and value creation. Instead of competing in saturated markets or "red oceans", where businesses fight for market share, the Blue Ocean Strategy encourages entrepreneurs to explore untapped markets or "blue oceans" that offer growth potential and minimal competition.

First used by: W Chan Kim and Renée Mauborgne, who introduced the concept in their 2005 book *Blue Ocean Strategy: How to Create Uncontested Market Space and Make the Competition Irrelevant*.

Practical aspects: Entrepreneurs can use various tools and techniques associated with the Blue Ocean Strategy to identify and create new value propositions, focusing on differentiation and low cost:

1. Strategy Canvas: This tool visually represents a company's current strategy compared to its

competitors. By plotting key factors on a graph, entrepreneurs can identify areas where they can create a unique value proposition and differentiate themselves from the competition.

2. Four Actions Framework: This framework helps entrepreneurs evaluate their business model by examining four key areas:
    a. Eliminate: Identify factors the industry takes for granted but can be removed to reduce costs or complexity.
    b. Reduce: Determine factors that can be scaled back or minimised to create cost savings or improve efficiency.
    c. Raise: Identify areas where the business can improve or increase value to customers.
    d. Create: Determine new factors that can be introduced to differentiate the business and create new demand.

Real-world examples:

1. Cirque du Soleil: By reimagining the traditional circus experience, Cirque du Soleil applied the Blue Ocean Strategy to create a unique and innovative entertainment offering. They eliminated animal acts and costly star performers, reduced reliance on traditional circus acts, raised production value with elaborate sets and costumes and created a new theatrical experience that combined elements of theatre, dance and acrobatics. This approach allowed them to tap into an uncontested market space and attract new audiences.

2. Southwest Airlines: Southwest Airlines employed the Blue Ocean Strategy to create a new market in the airline industry. They eliminated non-essential services like in-flight meals and seat assignments, reduced turnaround times, raised customer service standards and created a new low-cost, point-to-point air travel model. This strategy allowed Southwest to differentiate itself from traditional airlines and capture a new market segment of price-sensitive travellers.
3. Dyson: The vacuum cleaner manufacturer Dyson applied the Blue Ocean Strategy to revolutionise the home cleaning market. They eliminated the need for vacuum bags, reduced maintenance costs, raised suction power with innovative technology and created a new design aesthetic that differentiated their products from competitors. This approach allowed Dyson to create a new market space and attract customers who wanted more than traditional vacuum cleaners.

The Blue Ocean Strategy is an effective model for entrepreneurs looking to break free from intense competition and explore new market opportunities. By focusing on innovation, value creation and differentiation, businesses can attract new customers, create uncontested market spaces and achieve sustainable growth.

Growth Hacking: A Detailed Overview

Purpose: Growth Hacking is a model that focuses on rapid experimentation and data-driven decision-making to identify a business's most effective growth strategies. By utilising a combination of marketing, analytics and product development techniques, growth hacking aims to quickly test, measure and optimise growth strategies, emphasising scalability and cost-effective growth, especially for start-ups and small businesses.

First used by: Sean Ellis, who coined the term "growth hacking" in 2010 to describe some start-ups' unconventional marketing tactics and mindset to achieve rapid growth.

Practical aspects: Entrepreneurs and growth hackers employ a variety of techniques to drive growth in their businesses. Some critical aspects of growth hacking include:

1. Data-driven decision-making: Growth hackers use analytics tools and data to measure the impact of their strategies, allowing them to make informed decisions about which tactics are working and which need adjustment.
2. Rapid experimentation: By testing multiple tactics simultaneously or in quick succession, growth hackers can identify the most effective strategies and iterate on them to improve their impact. This process involves creating hypotheses, designing experiments, analysing results and learning from the outcomes.
3. Product/market fit: Growth hackers focus on finding a strong product/market fit – the point where a product meets the needs and desires of a specific market segment. Achieving product/market fit is essential for driving sustainable growth.
4. Virality: Growth hackers often explore strategies encouraging virality, such as referral programs, social sharing and word-of-mouth marketing. By tapping into network effects, businesses can accelerate growth and expand their reach organically.

Real-world examples:

1. Dropbox: Dropbox implemented a growth hacking strategy that focused on user referrals. By offering additional storage space as a reward for referring friends, Dropbox was able to increase sign-ups and grow its user base exponentially. The company also streamlined its onboarding process and made sharing files easy, contributing to its rapid growth.
2. Airbnb: Airbnb used growth hacking tactics to scale their business by leveraging Craigslist, a popular classified ads platform. They built a tool that allowed Airbnb hosts to cross-post their listings on Craigslist, tapping into a more extensive user base and driving traffic back to Airbnb. This strategy and other growth hacks, such as professional photography for listings, helped Airbnb become a dominant player in the home-sharing market.
3. Hotmail: Hotmail is an early example of growth hacking, where a simple but effective tactic drove rapid user acquisition. By adding a "Get your free email at Hotmail" message to the bottom of every email sent by its users, Hotmail was able to turn its users into promoters, leading to millions of sign-ups in a short period.

Growth hacking is a powerful approach for entrepreneurs looking to drive rapid business growth. Businesses can unlock new growth opportunities and scale their operations quickly and efficiently by focusing on data-driven decision-making, rapid experimentation and innovative tactics.

Agile Methodology: A Detailed Overview

Purpose: The Agile Methodology is an iterative and incremental approach to project management that emphasises flexibility, collaboration and customer feedback. Initially developed for software development projects, Agile has since been adopted across various industries to manage projects more efficiently and adapt quickly to changing requirements.

First used by: Software developers, as outlined in the Agile Manifesto (2001), which sought to improve traditional project management practices by prioritising individuals, interactions, working solutions and customer collaboration over rigid processes and documentation.

Practical aspects: Agile methodologies, such as Scrum and Kanban, offer entrepreneurs an effective way to manage projects by focusing on short development cycles, frequent feedback and continuous improvement:

1. Scrum: A popular Agile framework, Scrum organises work into time-boxed iterations called Sprints, typically lasting 2–4 weeks. Teams plan, develop and review work during each Sprint, with daily stand-up meetings to discuss progress and address any roadblocks. Key roles in Scrum include the Product Owner (responsible for the product vision and prioritising work), the Scrum Master (responsible for facilitating the process and removing obstacles) and the Development Team (responsible for delivering the work).
2. Kanban: Another Agile methodology, Kanban focuses on visualising work and optimising the flow of tasks through various stages of completion. Teams use a Kanban board to track work items, moving them through columns representing different stages (e.g. To-Do, In Progress, Done) as they are completed.

Kanban emphasises limiting work in progress (WIP) to prevent bottlenecks and ensure a smooth flow of tasks.

Real-world examples:

1. Spotify: The music streaming company Spotify has implemented Agile methodologies, including Scrum and Kanban, to manage its product development and engineering teams. Using Agile, Spotify can quickly respond to user feedback, iterate on its product offerings and maintain a competitive edge in the fast-paced tech industry.
2. IBM: A global technology company, adopted Agile methodologies to improve its software development processes and accelerate the delivery of new products and services. Agile has allowed IBM to reduce development cycles, enhance team collaboration and increase customer satisfaction.
3. Philips: A multinational technology corporation, implemented Agile methodologies to streamline its product development processes and quickly bring innovative healthcare solutions to the market. Agile has enabled Philips to respond more to market needs, improve cross-functional collaboration and enhance customer value.

The Agile Methodology offers entrepreneurs a flexible and collaborative approach to project management, making it well-suited for fast-paced, dynamic business environments. By adopting Agile methodologies like Scrum and Kanban, businesses can improve their ability to adapt to changing requirements, enhance teamwork and deliver customer value more efficiently.

APPENDIX F

A GUIDE TO SOFTWARE SELECTION

Something I draw attention to in a few places in this book is the importance of selecting the right software to support the essential elements of a new business. The following step-by-step guide should help you identify, evaluate and choose the most suitable software for your business.

Before you start looking for software solutions, make a list of your business's essential functions and requirements. Consider aspects like project management, customer relationship management (CRM), marketing automation, accounting and inventory management.

Research available options: Search for software solutions that cater to your industry and specific needs. Browse online reviews, ask for recommendations from fellow entrepreneurs, or consult industry-specific forums and social media groups for suggestions.

Shortlist software solutions: Based on your research, create a shortlist of software solutions that meet your business's requirements. Aim to have 3–5 options for further evaluation.

Evaluate software solutions using key metrics: To make an informed decision, consider the following key metrics:

a) Features and functionality: Make sure the software covers all your essential requirements and offers additional features that can benefit your business. Compare the features of each solution against your list of essential needs and look for case studies or testimonials from companies like yours to see how the software has helped them. Look for features that could improve your business operations or give you a competitive edge.
b) Ease of use: The software should be user-friendly, with an intuitive interface and a minimal learning curve for your team. Assess the user interface through demos or trials to determine if it's intuitive and user-friendly. Seek reviews or feedback from current users to gauge their satisfaction with the software's usability; organisations like Gartner often give you free access to compare software offerings. Finally, select solutions that offer training resources such as tutorials, webinars, or a comprehensive knowledge base to help your team become proficient quickly.
c) Customisability: A flexible software solution that can be tailored to your specific business processes will help you streamline operations. Inquire about customisation options, such as custom fields, forms, reports, or workflows. Determine if the software has an open API (Application Programming Interface) that allows for more advanced customisations or integrations with other tools. Consider choosing software that offers industry-specific templates or modules to streamline your implementation and configuration.
d) Scalability: As your business grows, the software should be able to accommodate your expanding

needs without significant upgrades or additional costs. Seek solutions offering multiple pricing tiers or plans, allowing you to upgrade or add features as your business grows but be aware of accelerating costs to use it. In addition, ensure the software can handle an increasing number of users, transactions, or data without performance issues. Ideally, opt for cloud-based solutions that automatically scale resources to accommodate your growing needs and provide accessible routes to upgrade.

e) Integration: Evaluate how well the software integrates with other tools and systems you already use or plan to use. Verify that it can integrate with the tools and platforms you already use, such as email, calendar, or accounting systems. Next, check the solution's integration capabilities, including native integrations, third-party apps, or compatibility with Zapier or similar connections. Finally, assess the ease of setting up and maintaining integrations, as this can impact your team's efficiency and final spending.

f) Support: Check the availability and quality of customer support, including response times, communication channels and access to training resources. Check the software provider's support channels like email, phone, chat, or forums. Look for providers that offer 24/7 support or have a strong reputation for responding quickly and effectively to customer inquiries. Read reviews or testimonials to learn about the quality of the support provided by the vendor.

g) Pricing: Analyse the cost of the software, considering factors like subscription fees, setup costs and potential hidden charges. Compare each software solution's pricing plans to determine which fits your budget. Calculate the total cost of ownership (TCO), factoring in setup fees, subscription costs and any additional costs for training, support, or upgrades. Seek out transparent pricing structures without hidden fees or long-term contracts that could lock you into a solution that may not fit your business best.

Request demos or trials: Contact the software providers to request demonstrations or free trials to get hands-on experience with the software. This will help you gauge the software's performance and usability.

Solicit feedback from your team: Involve your team members in the evaluation process, as they will use the software daily. Gather their feedback and opinions on the shortlisted options.

Make the final decision: Taking into account your research, key metrics evaluation, hands-on experience and team feedback, select the software that best meets your business needs.

Implement the software: Once you've decided, work with the software provider to implement the solution in your business. Allocate time for training and onboarding to ensure a smooth transition for your team.

Remember, choosing the right software is crucial for the success and efficiency of your new business. Take your time, evaluate your options thoroughly and make an informed decision to set your business up for success.

APPENDIX G

RECOMMENDED READING AND RESOURCES

As you embark on your entrepreneurial journey, continuous learning is essential for growth and success. *50 Golden Rules* provide an excellent foundation for any aspiring entrepreneur, but you must delve deeper into the vast ocean of knowledge and wisdom available to truly excel. This appendix contains a carefully curated list of books, articles and resources to help you gain further insights into entrepreneurship.

Books

The Lean Startup by Eric Ries: A modern classic, *The Lean Startup* introduces the concept of iterating and validating your business ideas using minimal resources, which has become a fundamental principle in today's fast-paced business landscape.

Zero to One by Peter Thiel: Peter Thiel, the co-founder of PayPal, shares his thoughts on how to build truly innovative businesses by focusing on creating something entirely new instead of improving existing models.

The E-Myth Revisited by Michael E Gerber: This book breaks down the myths surrounding entrepreneurship and provides a roadmap for building a successful and scalable business.

The Hard Thing About Hard Things by Ben Horowitz: Drawing on his experience as a CEO and venture capitalist, Ben Horowitz offers honest and insightful advice on navigating the challenges entrepreneurs face.

Good to Great by Jim Collins: Collins presents a comprehensive study of companies that made the leap from good to great and identifies the factors that contributed to their success.

The 7 Habits of Highly Effective People by Stephen R Covey: A timeless classic, this book covers the habits and principles that will help you become a more effective leader and entrepreneur.

The Innovator's Dilemma by Clayton M Christensen: Christensen introduces the concept of disruptive innovation, which has become a cornerstone of modern business strategy.

Blue Ocean Strategy by W Chan Kim and Renée Mauborgne: This book presents a framework for identifying uncontested market spaces and creating new demand rather than competing in saturated markets.

The Four Steps to the Epiphany by Steve Blank: Blank's book provides a practical approach to customer development, laying the groundwork for the Lean Start-up methodology.

The Personal MBA by Josh Kaufman: This book offers a comprehensive overview of essential business concepts and principles without needing an expensive MBA program.

The Art of the Start 2.0 by Guy Kawasaki: Guy Kawasaki shares his insights on starting a business, from creating a product to launching it into the market.

Shoe Dog by Phil Knight: Nike co-founder Phil Knight shares the story of his entrepreneurial journey and the lessons he learned along the way.

The Power of Broke by Daymond John: FUBU founder and Shark Tank investor Daymond John explains how a lack of resources can be a powerful motivator for entrepreneurs.

The $100 Start-up by Chris Guillebeau: This book showcases a range of successful micro businesses that started with minimal capital, demonstrating that anyone can become an entrepreneur.

Grit: The Power of Passion and Perseverance by Angela Duckworth: Psychologist Angela Duckworth explores spirit, an essential trait for entrepreneurs, and how it can be cultivated.

Angel Think: The Founders Guide to How Business Angels Think and How to Raise Money from Them by Phil McSweeney: This book provides founders with valuable insights about fundraising from business angels when they are first starting.

Go It Alone by Geoff Burch: This book provides superb insights, helping the reader to take their first steps in entrepreneurship, even if they want to be a "one-person-band". Written in Geoff's provocative and anecdotal style, it is a "must read".

Anyone Can Do It: Building Coffee Republic from Our Kitchen Table by Sahar and Bobby Hashemi: This is the book that inspired me to start my first business. Written in Sahar's approachable, informative style, the book contains a recipe for success when you are starting. It is also a very readable story.

Articles

The Five Competitive Forces That Shape Strategy by Michael E Porter: This article introduces Porter's Five Forces, a framework for analysing the competitive landscape of any industry.

The Innovator's Solution by Clayton M Christensen: A follow-up to *The Innovator's Dilemma*, this article offers solutions for dealing with disruptive innovation.

How to Start a Startup by Paul Graham: Y Combinator founder Paul Graham shares valuable insights and tips for those looking to start their businesses.

10,000 Hours with Reid Hoffman by Ben Casnocha: An insightful interview with LinkedIn's co-founder, discussing entrepreneurship, risk-taking and the importance of building a network.

Podcasts

How I Built This with Guy Raz: This podcast features interviews with successful entrepreneurs, sharing the stories behind their businesses and the challenges they faced along the way.

The Tim Ferriss Show: Tim Ferriss interviews high-profile individuals, extracting their habits, routines and insights that can be applied to entrepreneurship and personal development.

StartUp Podcast: A series documenting the journey of starting a business from scratch, providing an inside look at the realities of entrepreneurship.

The Ed Mylett Show: Ed Mylett interviews high-performing individuals from various fields, sharing their stories and success strategies that can be applied to entrepreneurship.

The Smart Passive Income Podcast: Pat Flynn discusses strategies for building online businesses and creating passive income streams.

The Indicator from Planet Money: This short-format podcast by NPR offers quick insights into work, business, the economy and everything in between.

Masters of Scale with Reid Hoffman: LinkedIn co-founder Reid Hoffman interviews successful entrepreneurs and business leaders, exploring how they scaled their businesses.

Online Resources

Coursera.org: Offers a variety of entrepreneurship-focused courses taught by professors from leading universities.

TED Talks: These inspiring talks cover many topics, including entrepreneurship, innovation and personal growth.

Harvard Business Review: HBR offers many articles, case studies, and resources on various entrepreneurship, management, and leadership aspects.

Y Combinator's Startup School: An online, free-to-attend programme that provides guidance and resources for entrepreneurs looking to start and scale their businesses.

Entrepreneur.com: A leading platform for entrepreneurs featuring news, advice and success stories from the business world.

Inc.com: Inc. offers practical advice, tools and services for entrepreneurs and profiles of successful start-ups and small businesses.

VentureBeat: A technology-focused publication providing news and insights on start-ups, venture capital and emerging industries.

SCORE.org: A non-profit organisation providing accessible business mentoring, advice and resources for entrepreneurs.

Sba.gov: The US Small Business Administration offers resources, guides and funding opportunities for entrepreneurs and small businesses.

AngelList: A platform for start-ups to connect with investors, find employees and discover resources to help grow their businesses.

UK Business Angels Association (UKBAA): The UKBAA is the national trade association for angel and early-stage investment in the UK. Their website (www.ukbaa.org.uk) provides a directory of angel groups, as well as resources and events related to angel investing.

APPENDIX H

USEFUL TOOLS AND SOFTWARE FOR ENTREPRENEURS

As an experienced entrepreneur, I know first-hand how the right tools and software can make all the difference in managing your business efficiently. This appendix is designed to provide a comprehensive list of useful tools and software that will help you streamline your operations, improve productivity and boost the growth of your entrepreneurial journey.

Project Management and Collaboration Tools:

- Trello: A flexible, visual tool for organising projects and tasks.
- Asana: A robust project management platform for teams.
- Basecamp: An all-in-one project management and team collaboration tool.
- Slack: A messaging app for teams, with integrations to many other tools.
- Microsoft Teams: A communication and collaboration platform with built-in Office suite tools.

Customer Relationship Management (CRM) Software:

- Salesforce: A cloud-based CRM platform for sales, service and marketing.
- HubSpot: A comprehensive inbound marketing, sales and CRM suite.
- Zoho CRM: A CRM platform for managing sales, marketing and customer support.

Accounting and Financial Management Software:

- QuickBooks: A comprehensive accounting software for small businesses.
- Xero: A cloud-based accounting platform with a focus on automation and collaboration.
- FreshBooks: A user-friendly invoicing and expense-tracking solution.

Email Marketing and Automation Tools:

- Mailchimp: A popular email marketing platform with automation capabilities.
- ActiveCampaign: A marketing automation platform with advanced segmentation and targeting.
- ConvertKit: A streamlined email marketing tool tailored for creators and small businesses.

Social Media Management Tools:

- Hootsuite: A platform for managing multiple social media accounts and scheduling posts.
- Buffer: A tool for scheduling and publishing social media content across various platforms.

- Sprout Social: A social media management tool with in-depth analytics and reporting features.

Website and E-commerce Platforms:

- WordPress: A flexible and widely used website building and content management system.
- Shopify: A powerful e-commerce platform for creating and managing online stores.
- Squarespace: A user-friendly website builder with templates for various industries.

Analytics and Data Visualisation Tools:

- Google Analytics: A popular tool for tracking website traffic and user behaviour.
- Tableau: A data visualisation software for creating interactive and shareable reports.
- Mixpanel: A product analytics platform for tracking user interactions and engagement.

Customer Support and Helpdesk Software:

- Zendesk: A customer service platform for managing support tickets and interactions.
- Freshdesk: A helpdesk software with multichannel support and automation features.
- Intercom: A customer messaging platform for support, marketing and sales.

Time Management and Productivity Apps:

- Todoist: A task management app for organising and prioritising daily tasks.
- Evernote: A note-taking app for capturing ideas, documents and images.
- RescueTime: A time-tracking software for monitoring and improving productivity.

Design and Video Editing Tools:

- Canva: A user-friendly graphic design tool with templates for various formats.
- Adobe Creative Cloud: A suite of professional design and video editing applications.
- InVideo: An online video editor for creating promotional and social media videos.

Remember, every business is unique, and you may not require all the above mentioned tools. Instead, choose the ones that best suit your needs and help you achieve your entrepreneurial goals. As your business grows, you may need to explore additional tools and software to support your growing business.

APPENDIX I

GLOSSARY OF ENTREPRENEURSHIP TERMS

As an experienced entrepreneur, I understand the importance of familiarising oneself with the jargon and terms used in entrepreneurship. This glossary aims to provide an overview of essential terms to help you easily navigate the entrepreneurial landscape. Here are some keywords you'll come across.

Accelerator: A time-limited support program for start-ups that offers mentorship, education and resources to help them scale their businesses rapidly.

Angel Investor: A high-net-worth individual who invests in start-ups, often in exchange for equity or convertible debt.

Bootstrapping: Funding a business using personal savings or revenue generated from the company's operations.

Break-even Point: The point at which a business's revenues equal costs, resulting in neither profit nor loss.

Business Model: A company's strategy for generating revenue and sustaining its operations, including its target market, value proposition and revenue streams.

Cash Flow: The movement of money in and out of a business, typically measured over a specific period.

Churn Rate: The rate customers stop doing business with a company, usually expressed as a percentage.

Convertible Debt: A short-term loan that can be converted into equity later, usually upon a predetermined event, such as a funding round.

Crowdfunding: A method of raising capital by soliciting small contributions from many individuals, typically through online platforms.

Disruption: The process of introducing an innovative product, service, or business model that significantly alters how a market or industry operates.

Elevator Pitch: A concise, persuasive summary of a business idea that can be presented in the time it takes to ride an elevator.

Equity: Ownership in a company, typically represented by shares or stocks.

Exit Strategy: A plan for how an entrepreneur or investor will realise a return on their investment, such as through an acquisition or an initial public offering (IPO).

Freemium: A business model that offers essential services for free while charging for premium features or additional services.

Growth Hacking: A marketing approach focused on rapid experimentation and data-driven decision-making to optimise growth and user acquisition.

Intellectual Property (IP): Creations of the mind, such as inventions, designs and artistic works, protected by patents, copyrights, or trademarks.

Lean Start-up: A methodology for building businesses and products that emphasises rapid experimentation, customer feedback and iterative development.

Market Validation: The process of determining whether there is sufficient demand for a product or service before investing significant resources into its development.

Minimum Viable Product (MVP): A simplified version of a product or service that includes only its core features, allowing it to be tested with early adopters and refined based on their feedback.

Pivot: A strategic change in a company's direction or focus, typically in response to market feedback or changing conditions.

Scaling: The process of growing a business by expanding its operations, customer base, or revenue streams.

Seed Capital: The initial funding used to launch a start-up, often provided by the founders, friends, family, or angel investors.

Series A, B, C, etc.: Various rounds of funding for a start-up, each typically involving a higher valuation and more significant investment than the previous one.

Start-up: A newly established business venture typically focused on addressing a specific market opportunity or problem through innovative products or services.

Term Sheet: A non-binding agreement outlining the key terms of an investment.

Traction: Demonstrable progress in a start-up's growth, customer acquisition, or market penetration, often used to attract investors or partners.

Unique Selling Proposition (USP): The factor that sets a product or service apart from its competitors, making it more attractive to customers.

User Acquisition: The process of attracting and converting new users or customers to a product or service.

Valuation: The estimated worth of a business, typically determined by factors such as revenue, growth potential and market share.

Value Proposition: The unique combination of features, benefits and pricing a product or service offers to its target market.

Venture Capital (VC): A form of financing provided by firms or funds to start-ups and early-stage companies with high growth potential in exchange for equity.

Vesting: The process by which employees or founders gradually earn the right to own shares or stock options in a company over time.

Viral Coefficient: A measure of how effectively a product or service spreads through word-of-mouth, often calculated as the average number of new users generated by each existing user.

Working Capital: The difference between a company's current assets and current liabilities, used to evaluate its liquidity and financial health.

By familiarising yourself with these entrepreneurship terms, you'll be better equipped to understand the concepts and strategies presented in this book. In addition, you will be able to hold your own in conversations with fellow entrepreneurs and potential investors.

As you continue your entrepreneurial journey, remember that learning the language of entrepreneurship is just the first step. It's essential to internalise the lessons and advice in the book and gain real-world experience to fully grasp what it means to be a successful entrepreneur.

ABOUT THE AUTHOR

Garry Mansell is a seasoned entrepreneur and business leader with over 40 years of experience in procurement, supply chain management, systems development and entrepreneurship. Garry has built and led thriving businesses throughout his career, leveraging his extensive knowledge and expertise to create innovative solutions in diverse industries.

Garry's first business, Freight Traders, was launched during the dot-com boom in 1999 and quickly became one of Europe's leading freight exchanges. In 2006, he orchestrated the merger of Freight Traders with the emerging Swedish company Trade Extensions. As CEO, Garry led the newly formed business to become the undisputed leader in sourcing optimisation. His strategic vision and leadership culminated in the company's successful sale to Coupa Software in 2016.

Since then, Garry has actively invested in and served as a non-executive director and board advisor for various small and medium-sized businesses across multiple sectors, including digital marketing, healthcare, animal nutrition, artificial intelligence and machine learning.

In addition to his entrepreneurial achievements, Garry is a Fellow of the Chartered Institute of Logistics and Transport and a Fellow of the Chartered Institute of Procurement and Supply, where he also serves as a Global Board Trustee.

Garry's passion for entrepreneurship and business success led him to author his first book, *Simplify to Succeed*, 2022, and which quickly became an Amazon bestseller. Building on the success of his first book, Garry has now penned *50 Golden Rules: A Beginner's Guide to Entrepreneurship* to continue sharing his knowledge and insights with the next generation of aspiring entrepreneurs.

Drawing from his wealth of experience, Garry offers readers valuable lessons, practical advice, and real-world examples to help them navigate the exciting and often challenging world of entrepreneurship. His commitment to fostering a thriving entrepreneurial community and empowering others to achieve their dreams is evident on every page of this guide.